A Guide for Black Chokeberry Edibles and Sundries

is for Aronia

CHERYL
SAKER

ISBN: 0615441661
ISBN-13: 9780615441665

To my dear husband, Jim, and sons, Jamie and Rob, for

their endless support and encouragement.

Table of Contents

⌘   ⌘   ⌘

Preface

"What do you do with them?" That's the question first-time tasters of *Aronia* berries ask most often. It is pretty obvious from the first bite that these are not your typical pop-in-the-mouth fruits. As friends and family asked this question repeatedly, I realized the need for a guide to answer this question so everyone could benefit from this berry's health qualities.

My own journey leading to my passion for this berry has been a culmination of life events. It seems that when we are in the midst of "living," we exist in robot mode, merely trying to make it from one day to the next. But, upon reaching a stage of life called "maturity," which is accompanied by discount cards and special sale days, you see how all the pieces of life's puzzle fit together to create your identity and unique journey.

Life for me began in the midst of World War II. My grandparents grew vegetables in their "victory gardens" and shared their bounty with neighbors and family. Luckily my elementary school had a summer project in which I eagerly participated—gardening. My grandfather would sit and offer guidance as I planted and weeded all summer.

The generations of my parents and grandparents had so much to offer. Their experiences in the Great Depression gave them an appreciation for everything, big and small. Food was never wasted, leading to some interesting concoctions for dinner. The more creative the cook, the more unique the food product became. As a result, I learned during my childhood to stretch the imagination and to try new food combinations. Unfortunately, we also had to clean our plates, because wastefulness was not in the family vocabulary.

Fortunately for me, I had a dear aunt to teach me how to cook when I was young. Even before I was as tall as the table top, she was letting me help her in the kitchen. She and my uncle made meals an experience. We did not have store containers on the table or paper napkins. Meals were social times when we talked about a variety of topics, all planned to encourage my ideas and creativity.

During my secondary-school years, we lived in the country on acreage and, as a result, the garden became much larger! I thought it was strange that we mixed flowers with vegetables, but my family did not believe in using chemicals, so I learned that the smell of certain plants would keep insects away from our valuable crop. (Amazingly, this was during the fifties and into the sixties and before Rachel Carson wrote *Silent Spring*.) Gardening chores now expanded into freezer and canning duties. In addition to the root cellar, we had three full freezers and rows of canned goods on the shelves.

When college years beckoned, I went off to pursue studies in architecture. There was one minor problem: I was a girl! Although I had taken the appropriate math and science classes for this path, my professors suggested I look at interior design. But, that didn't appeal to me. Finally, I realized I always liked to cook, and perhaps a major with food science and nutrition would be a good fit.

Marriage followed college. My partner, who has been my best friend for over forty-five years, came from a similar background raising animals, gardening, and participating in 4-H activities. Throughout our marriage, we have always maintained a garden in one form or another. There is always a full freezer and canned vegetables on the pantry shelves. Our sons grew up loving whole grains, vegetables, and fruits, and enjoying family meal time. They also learned to garden and to appreciate the taste of fresh vegetables and fruits.

When the date for retirement from teaching came closer and closer, I knew that I would never fit into the soap-opera-watching lifestyle. At the same time, my doctor was throwing out phrases such as "genetic predisposition to...," so my research began into foods that would help ward off these looming diseases—and there it was: *Aronia melanocarpa.* Together with my family, we now tend to over two thousand *Aronia* bushes. And I began to explore ways to use the berries. My nutrition background taught me that whole food consumption far outweighs the advantages of a pill or extract. Thus began my journey to develop recipes and methodologies for using the berry while protecting its health attributes.

⌘　⌘　⌘

An Introduction to Aronia

Several images pop into our minds when we think of the color purple. First we envision a hue formed by mixing blue and red. Perhaps we saw the movie with the same name. Or a vision of the jolly and bouncy dinosaur loved by children is dancing around. Is it a thought of royalty? For some it may be a memory from the past of the purple people eater. Could it be the color to wear when you are old? Or is it the plump, highly nutritious berry *Aronia melanocarpa*? Familiarity occurs with this entire list except for the last item. Yet for those involved with nutrition and health trends, *Aronia melanocarpa* is gaining much-deserved attention as the purple of choice.

Aronia melanocarpa, referred to commonly as black chokeberry, is a deciduous shrub grown in many regions of the United States. Native to the Great Lakes and northeast United States, it is found as far south as northern sections of Texas and Florida, parts of the Appalachian Mountains, west along the Missouri River corridor, and along the western coast in the states of Oregon and Washington. Our neighbors to the north grow the berry from Nova Scotia to Ontario. It is a member of the Rosaceae (rose) family and, depending on the cultivar, can grow from three to twelve feet tall.

Aronia melanocarpa is a hardy and tolerant plant. The best berry production occurs when the plant has full sun and moist but well-drained soil which is slightly acidic. Berries form on clusters and mature in late summer when they have developed their beautiful purple hue. For food purposes, the cultivars grown most widely are 'Viking,' 'Nero,' 'Elata,' and 'Aron.' While all cultivars produce berries with antioxidant qualities, those developed for food production generally are more palatable and provide more juice. However, the cultivars with less juice are suitable for dehydration and used in baked goods and pet foods.

This amazing berry has traveled the world. *Aronia melanocarpa* berries and leaves were used by Native Americans for medicinal purposes to treat colds and other ailments. They included the berry in their daily diet for health. Europeans who settled in the New World found the berry to be astringent and chalky in taste, thus giving it the nickname "choke berry." Introduced to Russia in the nineteenth century, it was developed into commercial cultivation in the late 1940s and used as an antihypertensive herbal drug. Commercial cultivation spread to Sweden in the late 1980s, and the berry is now grown widely in Ukraine, Poland, Germany, the Baltics, Russia, Czech Republic, and Slovakia. It also has been introduced to Japan. Some estimates suggest Poland is the world leader in *Aronia* production with tens of thousands of berries harvested each year.

In addition to being extraordinary *Aronia* producers, the European *Aronia* community has been the research leader of this berry's health benefit potential. Studies recently have commenced in the United States with animal subjects that show promise with *Aronia* in the diet. A Web-based search of *Aronia* will take you to articles touting the antioxidant, antimutagenic, cardioprotective, antihyperglycemic, and hepatoprotective qualities. To the average consumer this is quite a mouthful. But we do know that this berry has very high concentrations of phytochemicals called anthocyanins.

Aronia's chemical properties provide an extremely high antioxidant value, referred to as the oxygen radical absorbing capacity (ORAC). ORAC values of *Aronia* are reportedly five times greater than blueberries, eight times greater than cranberries, and four times greater than lingonberries. This is an important fact to know because our bodies are constantly being exposed to stressors which affect the well-being of our cells similar to salt being corrosive to metal. Regardless of the stressor, good or bad, the effect is the same. The antioxidative qualities of *Aronia* can reduce the rate of the oxidation process. Also, several research studies note the inhibited growth of various cancer cells when consuming this berry daily.

Europeans have an even broader appreciation for the power of *Aronia* and advertise the berry as a tremendous boost to the immune system for a broad spectrum of conditions, including brain dysfunctions (senile dementia, Parkinson's disease), arterial plaque buildup, inflammatory diseases, and high blood pressure, to list a few.

Perhaps the best analogy for human *Aronia* consumption is to think of our bodies as cars. Like the car, our body can have a negative reaction to the oxidative process. *Aronia* has the capability of slowing down the oxidative process, similar to what wax does for our car. Daily consumption is a good preventative food for many conditions.

Since berries are a high-density food, nutritionists recommend whole berry consumption. In addition to the nutritive benefits, the whole berry provides a good source of fiber in the diet. Whole berries that are fresh, frozen, or dehydrated meet that criterion. The juicing process creates the juice and pomace (solid matter), so it is important to find a way to incorporate both into the diet.

Aronia berries can be used in a variety of recipes. However, to maintain the high level of antioxidants, the food processing methods need to maintain low temperatures for as short a period as possible. Some of the recipes in this cookbook use the raw berry or juice without high heat, allowing the full nutritional properties of the berry to be ingested. No study has indicated any toxicity with *Aronia* for humans or pets. So enjoy!

Aronia does have an astringent taste, so the berries are used mostly as a food additive ingredient rather than a singular consumption food. Also, the berries seem to be more flavorful after a cold treatment in the freezer. Many people find that with a slow introduction to the berry in food combinations, they develop a taste for the berry. Some actually report a craving for the berry. The following lists suggest some ways to start adding *Aronia* berries to your diet.

Whole Fresh/Frozen Berry
- For recipes using cherries or cranberries, substitute *Aronia* berries for one-quarter or one-third of the amount used.
- Stir into cooked cereals, such as oatmeal.
- Stir a tablespoon into fruited yogurt.

Dehydrated Berry Bits
- Add to any baked goods, such as oatmeal cookies, muffins, pound cakes, pancakes, etc.
- Steep with green or white teas.

Juice
- Add to purchased orange juice, lemonade, and apple juice.
- Substitute for a portion or all of the liquids in sauce recipes and baked goods (the finished product will be purple).

Pomace from Juice Processing

- Sprinkle on cereals or add to smoothies.
- Sprinkle a teaspoon on pet food.

Aronia berries are becoming readily available, especially throughout the growing regions where they are found in farmers' markets and pick-your-own orchards. Consumers who do not have access to these markets can often find them at local organic and/or health food stores. If not, ask the store manager to consider adding them to the store's product line.

Several juice companies are using *Aronia* as an additive ingredient for coloring and antioxidant value. One nationwide company lists *Aronia* juice as the second ingredient in almost all of its juice blends. Read the ingredients on the label and you'll be surprised at the number of products that include *Aronia*.

⌘　⌘　⌘

Adding Aronia to Your Diet

Similar to food introduction with an infant, *Aronia* should be introduced in an appealing manner so individuals can acquire the taste and benefit from the healthful qualities. Many of the recipes contained in this book will appeal to young and old and will introduce the *Aronia* taste gradually.

Berry selection is important. Choose berries which are firm and plump with a beautiful deep purplish hue. The majority of the *Aronia* cultivars in the United States have berries that ripen over a two- or three-week period. If you are hand-picking your berries, you may find some on the cluster ready to pick but with neighbors that need more time. Berries which have overripened will look like dried raisins and are not desirable for human consumption. Let the birds enjoy them during the winter.

In addition to gradually introducing the taste of *Aronia* berries, it is important to maintain the integrity of the berry's anthocyanin levels. These can be destroyed by high pH, light exposure, or high temperature. Current research has demonstrated that conditions exist which can protect these qualities. Frozen berries and juice will not experience loss of anthocyanins. Similarly, products made with a food dehydrator will be less affected, especially if the drying process is on low heat. And, the same applies to use of a slow cooker on low heat. Baked products can benefit from being baked in a convection oven. The baking temperature for a convection oven is twenty-five degrees less than conventional baking, and the length of baking time is usually less. Another finding in the research indicates that the addition of citric acid helps to protect the anthocyanins by lowering the pH. Citric acid can easily be added with a citrus juice (orange, lime, lemon) or with a powder found in the canning supply aisle.

While this guide's intent is to identify uses for *Aronia*, consideration has been made to align with the Dietary Guidelines for Americans, 2010. Making the top of the recommendation list is to reduce sodium intake—salt. While some foods contain sodium naturally, the majority of our sodium intake comes from processed foods. Most of the recipes in this guide use little or no additional salt. While it may be tempting to add or increase salt in recipes, try adding more herbs or spices instead to enhance flavors. Another guideline recommendation is to increase nutrient-dense foods. Berries are definitely in this category. Unlike fats, sugars, and processed grains, berries can be part of your diet as often as you like. So, start eating and enjoying *Aronia* berries. Your vital organs will thank you for it!

⌘ ⌘ ⌘

Processing Methods for Aronia Berries

When processing *Aronia* berries, consideration must be made to minimize the berries' exposure to high heat, in order to maintain the antioxidant benefits of the berry. Storage availability is also an important consideration for berry processing. Ideal conditions are to process the berry and then store in the freezer for up to 12 months. Berry juice can be processed via canning, but the high heat from the water bath and/or pressure canner may destroy some of the antioxidant qualities. Thus, whether the berries are juiced or kept whole, your freezer is the best site for long-term storage. The freezer not only preserves the berries but heightens the sweetness. Basic processing methods addressed in this section include freezing, juicing, and dehydrating.

Freezing: This is the best method for whole berry storage. Once the berries have been cleaned and all stems and leaves removed, place the whole berries in a single layer on a parchment-paper-lined jellyroll pan (cookie sheet with sides). Place the pan in the freezer until the berries are frozen. Pack the frozen berries in freezer containers. Vacuum packing with a vacuum meal sealer is ideal. The frozen whole berries are firm and can withstand this process. By removing the excess air, you will use less space in the freezer. Mark all containers with the berry form and date and return to the freezer.

Frozen berries can be used in any recipe, but in most they will need to be thawed first at room temperature. This is especially important for jams/jellies, sauces, and baked goods. However, when a recipe requires chopped berries, it is best to chop them in the frozen state. They chop nicely without becoming mushy. If they seem to be too hard for your processor, let them rest for 10 minutes to thaw slightly.

Dehydrating Whole and/or Chopped Berries: There are benefits to dehydrating berries in the whole or chopped form. The health benefits remain, and the dried berry can be incorporated into baked goods without changing the color of the batter. The dehydrated berry is a great addition to trail mix, granola, and other recipes that do not require refrigeration. The cultivar of your berry will affect the time required for dehydration. 'Viking' and 'Nero' have almost twice the amount of juice compared to 'Autumn Magic' and other ornamental cultivars. Therefore, the latter cultivar requires less time for dehydration.

Since the skin of the berry is thick and waxy, the whole berry does not dehydrate completely. The skin needs to be cracked for the internal berry to dry consistently. A pretreatment eliminates this problem. These steps include the following:

- Blanch the berries in boiling water for 60 seconds and immerse in ice cold water immediately. This should crack the berry skin.
- Drain the berries in a strainer and pat them dry on a paper towel to remove excess water.
- Spread the berries on mesh dehydrator grids with openings small enough to prevent the berries from falling through.

Drying times will vary with the size of the berries and the dehydrator temperature. If you can regulate the temperature for the dehydrator, set it to 135°F and check the berries after 10 to 12 hours. If the dehydrator does not have a temperature regulator, it may take up to 12 to 14 hours for the berries to dry to a raisinlike consistency. Some people have used the oven for dehydrating berries. While this method can be used, most ovens have a minimum temperature setting around 170°F. A convection oven helps circulate air, but regardless of which oven you use (conventional or convection), the berries need to be turned frequently and watched closely. Also, if your only option is a conventional or convection oven, the chopped berry method would be best since the pieces are smaller and would dry more evenly and at a quicker rate.

Dehydrating Bits: Place fresh or frozen *Aronia* berries in a medium-sized bowl of a food processor with the metal blade attachment. Frozen berries chop more cleanly and do not create a mush. Pulse the blade to chop. If necessary, remove the lid from the food processor and scrape the sides of the processor wall to keep the berries down with the blades. Spread the chopped berries on a dehydrator mat. Place the mat in the dehydrator for approximately 10 to 12 hours. Or, if you have a dehydrator with a temperature regulator, set it to 135°F and dehydrate for 8 to 10 hours. The berries should be dry and somewhat pliable, like a raisin. Dehydrated berries are concentrated and give twice the amount of nutrients as an equal amount of fresh.

Juicing: During this process two products are created—the juice and a pomace. Pomace is the solid material, such as skin and seeds, that separates from the berry. Both products have nutritive value. Some studies indicate that the skin of the berry is extremely high in anthocyanin qualities. Therefore it is important to keep the pomace produced during juicing.

Berries can be juiced in an extractor or by hand. If using the extractor, a slight steaming before the juicing process helps soften the skin to release more of the skin's properties into the juice. The rice bowl of a steamer works well because it keeps all of the berry juice in the container. Place the berries in the steamer and steam for approximately 12 minutes. Let the berries cool slightly before processing. Follow the manufacturer's directions if using a juicer. For the hand method, it is helpful to use berries which have been chopped slightly in the food processor. Steam the chopped berries for 12 to 15 minutes and cool slightly before transferring them to a dampened jelly bag. A strainer with several layers of dampened cheesecloth can be used, too. The jelly bag or strainer should be placed over a deep bowl. Let the juice drip into the container for 2 to 3 hours undisturbed. Give the bag a gentle squeeze or use a spoon to press down on the berries to release additional juices. Although there will be some variance with the type of extractor used and the berry cultivar, 1½ pounds of berries should yield about 2 cups of juice. If you are fortunate enough to have an abundant supply of berries, it is advantageous to juice several pounds of berries in one sitting. The juice can be processed via canning, but to maintain the nutritive value, freezing is best. The vacuum packer/sealer works well with juice, too. First prepare the bags by sealing one end of the vacuum bag. Pour the juice into the bags, leaving at least 4 inches of bag at the top, and stack upright in a container to place in the freezer. Once the juice is frozen, the open end can be put into the vacuum sealer to complete the sealing. Two-cup bags are useful. They can be defrosted as needed and require minimal freezer space.

The remaining pomace can be frozen as is or dehydrated slightly. The dehydrated form can be sprinkled on yogurt, cereals, or even on a pet's food. Most pomace is quite dry and requires only about an hour in the dehydrator to remove any moisture. When dry place the pomace in an airtight jar and keep in the refrigerator to use as needed.

⌘　⌘　⌘

Breakfast

The most important meal of the day, breakfast, is often skipped or skimped. Hurried lifestyles necessitate planning for easy-to-grab foods to "break the fast." All or portions of the recipes in this section can be prepared ahead to facilitate minimal preparation at daybreak.

Smoothies

There is nothing easier to prepare for a nutritional energy boost for the day. Breakfast smoothies usually consist of three basic ingredients: liquid, yogurt, and fruit. Use these ingredients in a proportion of one-half part liquid, one part yogurt, and one part fruit. That said…anything goes. Personal taste and thickness preference should be the guide.

Liquid Options:
Apple or berry juice (can be part *Aronia* berry juice)
Milk, fat free or 1 percent
Soy milk, regular or lowfat; vanilla flavor is nice
Almond milk

Yogurt:
An easy way to incorporate yogurt into a smoothie is to pour the yogurt into an ice cube tray and put it in the freezer. When the cubes have frozen, place them in a freezer-proof container. They can be used as needed and give the smoothie a nice chill without the addition of ice cubes.

Use yogurt with an active culture and without gelatin added. Greek yogurt is fine, but because it is thicker it may require additional liquid to create the right consistency.

Fruit:
Use a mixture of berries that includes one-third *Aronia* berries. Berry mixtures are available in the freezer section without added sugar, and the *Aronia* easily

can be added. Other fruits to include are apples slices, banana chunks, mango, papaya, peaches, and other soft fruits. Citrus fruits are not recommended since they may interact with the dairy products.

Extras:

There are several ways to boost the nutritional level of the smoothie. A mere tablespoon of creamy peanut butter or almond butter, flax meal, barley grass, brewer's yeast, wheat germ, or nutritional supplements can be added.

Sweetener:

If vanilla yogurt and/or vanilla milk are used along with ripe berries, there is usually no need for added sweetener. If necessary, a tablespoon of honey, agave syrup, or pure maple syrup may be added to the mixture.

Basic Breakfast Smoothie—Serves 2
I cup yogurt
I cup berries, fresh or frozen, including 1/3 cup *Aronia* berries
½ cup milk or apple juice
I teaspoon honey or agave syrup

Place all ingredients in the blender. Process for 30–40 seconds. Taste and add more berries, milk, or sweetener if needed.

Peanut Butter and Jelly Smoothie—Makes 1¾ cups
I cup yogurt
I banana cut into chunks (if possible freeze ahead)
½ cup milk or milklike product
I tablespoon *Aronia* jelly(recipe in Jams and Jellies chapter)
I tablespoon peanut butter, creamy

Place all ingredients in the blender and process for 30–40 seconds. Taste and add more berries, milk, or sweetener if needed.

Cereals

Cereal and milk is a breakfast mainstay. For variety try something new. Make breakfast parfaits with layers of fruit, yogurt, and granola or muesli. The parfaits can be layered in plastic cups and kept in the freezer. Remove the night before for defrosting in the refrigerator. The parfait will be a nice frosty wake up in the morning. Or sprinkle a dish of yogurt with granola to add crunch and fiber. Top off frozen yogurt or ice cream with a spoonful or two. Replace the top crust of a fruit pie with a layer of granola.

The granola and muesli can be stored in bags or containers with tight-fitting lids. It is best to keep them in the refrigerator or freezer and remove as needed.

Granola for Health—Makes 8 cups
4 cups quick-cooking rolled oats
½ cup flaked or shredded coconut
¼ cup wheat germ
½ cup pumpkin seeds, shelled
½ cup sunflower seeds, shelled
¼ cup canola or corn oil
¼ teaspoon salt
½ cup honey or maple syrup (not maple-flavored corn syrup)
1½ teaspoons vanilla extract
½ cup *Aronia* berries, dehydrated
½ cup raisins or dates, chopped
½ cup pineapple, dried and chopped
½ cup apricots, dried and chopped

In a large mixing bowl, combine the first 5 ingredients. Toss until well mixed. In a smaller bowl mix the oil, salt, sweetener, and vanilla until well-blended. Mix into the dry mixture by tossing. Use a rubber spatula to scrape the sides and toss. Lightly grease a jellyroll pan or cookie sheet with sides, or use a silicone baking pan mat or parchment paper to line the pan. Spread the granola mixture onto the pan. Bake in an oven set at a low temperature of 250°F. Use a metal or silicone spatula to turn the granola every 15 minutes. Do this until the granola turns a golden brown, approximately 1 hour. Remove the pan and let cool. When completely cool, pour the granola into a very large bowl and add the last four ingredients—the dried fruits. Toss to blend. Store the granola in a container with a tight-fitting lid or freezer-proof bag and freeze.

Muesli—Makes about 10 cups
2 cups oats, steel cut
2 cups oats, rolled
1 cup walnuts, roughly chopped
1 cup *Aronia* berries, dehydrated and chopped
½ cup raisins or dates, chopped
½ cup apricots, dried and chopped
½ cup apples, dried slices cut into pieces
½ cup pumpkin seeds, shelled
½ cup flaxseeds

Mix all ingredients in a large bowl. Transfer to an airtight container and store in the refrigerator, or in the freezer if longer storage is needed. To serve cold, mix one part muesli with 1½ parts milk, soy milk, almond milk, apple juice, or water and allow to rest for about 15 minutes. To serve hot, combine equal amount of muesli and liquid and simmer on the range for 3–5 minutes or microwave on high for 3 minutes, stirring halfway through.

Granola Bars—Makes 16 bars
Some mornings require an easy "out-the-door" food to grab. Use the granola to make bars so there is no excuse for not starting the day out right.
1 tablespoon butter
¼ cup dark brown sugar
3 tablespoons maple syrup
3 tablespoons agave nectar or honey
2 teaspoons vanilla
2 cups *Aronia* granola(recipe in Breakfast chapter)
½ cup dark chocolate chips

Preheat oven to 300°F. Spray an 8x8-inch baking pan with cooking spray or coat lightly with butter or shortening.

Combine all ingredients except the vanilla, granola, and chocolate chips in a large saucepan. Heat on medium until the sugar dissolves, stirring constantly. Remove the pan from the heat and add the vanilla. Stir to combine thoroughly. In a medium bowl combine the granola with the chocolate chips. Slowly pour the liquid mixture over the granola/chocolate chips and stir until well blended. Press the mixture into the prepared baking pan. It is important to press the mixture into the pan. Since the mixture is sticky, it helps to moisten your hands with water and hand press the mixture.

Bake for 25 minutes. While the bars are semi-warm, use the end of a metal spatula to cut the squares, but do not remove until thoroughly cooled. Store in an airtight container.

Beverages

Beverages are a simple and practical way to incorporate *Aronia* into the daily diet. Add up to 1 cup of *Aronia* juice to 1 quart of bottled juices. Encourage children in the family to be "chemists" by recommending the type of main juice to use before adding the *Aronia* juice, and then have a vote to see which one is their favorite. Most juices are high in sugar, but with the addition of the *Aronia* juice, the sugar concentration is reduced per serving. Another advantage to using *Aronia* in beverages is the absence of heat (except for the tea and tisane recipes) so the healthful qualities are maintained. Most of these recipes can be modified for personal taste. Enjoy!

Tea

Frequently "tea" is used as a generic term for an infusion of dried herbs/ leaves and hot water. Yet an authentic tea is one made with the leaves from the *Camellia sinensis* plant. The curing method determines if it will be called white, black, green, or oolong. Teas are being recognized for health benefits, especially the white and green teas. Combining them with *Aronia* provides a double health benefit.

Aronia Tea Blend

1½ cups loose green or white tea leaves
Rind from two lemons, grated and dried (overnight on wax paper on the counter)
2–3 tablespoons mint leaves, dried and crumbled
2 tablespoons crystallized ginger, chopped fine
½ cup *Aronia* bits, dehydrated and finely chopped
Toss all ingredients to mix well, and store in an airtight container.

To serve:

Begin with fresh, filtered cold water and heat to 185°F. A sign that this stage is reached is the forming of a string of bubbles gently starting to rise to the top from the bottom. White and green teas will be bitter tasting if boiling water is used for steeping. On the plus side, though, the lower water temperature helps to maintain the antioxidant qualities to a better degree. Add 2–3 teaspoons of the tea blend to a tea ball or infuser. Pour the heated water over the tea and infuse to taste. Full leaf tea takes longer to infuse than a tea bag, so allow 2–4 minutes depending on taste preference. Remove the infuser or tea ball and enjoy hot or on ice!

Tisanes

A tisane is a refreshing beverage made with aromatic herbs. Some of the more popular herbs to use include bee balm, catnip, chamomile, ginger root, lavender flowers, lemongrass, lemon verbena, peppermint, rosemary, rose hips, and spearmint. Many of these herbs have long been used to aid digestion, calm the nerves, or energize the body.

For each cup of tisane you will need about 2 teaspoons of dried herbs or 3 teaspoons of fresh herbs. Dried herbs are more concentrated, which is why a lesser amount is needed. The difference is due to the dried herbs being concentrated. Add an additional teaspoon or tablespoon of dried *Aronia* bits to the mixture. Steep the herbal mixture with heated water (not boiling) for 4–8 minutes, depending on the preferred strength, and then strain. The tisane may be served hot or cold for a refreshing drink.

Aronia Juice Ice Cubes

An easy way to ice drinks and add the *Aronia* juice is to fill an ice cube mold with *Aronia* juice. The variety of molds available today is a fun way to add pizzazz to an ordinary beverage. Add the frozen cubes to iced tea, lemonade, or lemon-lime beverages.

Aronia Fizz

There are numerous carbonated beverages on the market that provide a base for *Aronia* juice. Italian sparkling mineral waters are ideal. Most are carbohydrate, fat, and calorie free with minimal sodium. Two tablespoons of *Aronia* juice topped off with the sparkling mineral water and a sprig of mint make a refreshing drink on a hot day.

Alcoholic Beverages
<u>Bitters</u>

An alcoholic beverage produced from an infusion of barks, herbs, roots, fruits, etc., bitters were used originally for medicinal purposes almost two hundred years ago. Since then, this mixture has entered the mixed-drink ingredient category. Uses included treating sailors' upset stomachs and were expanded to other ailments. Originally bitters were imbibed straight, but then were combined with soda or ginger ale to settle the stomach.

Bitters utilize three ingredient components: the bittering agent, the flavor, and the solution. The solution is usually an alcohol with the highest available proof. Vodka and gin mix well with *Aronia*, but a hardier bitter can be made with bourbon. The bittering agent is the *Aronia*, and the flavoring agent ranges from citrus to cardamom; this is the component that makes the unique taste for your bitter. Simplicity is the rule to follow when choosing the flavoring agent. Select no more than two flavors. Some combinations make wonderful choices, such as lemongrass and grated ginger or lemon peel and mint leaves. When the bitter recipe has been aged, it can be used with soda, lemonade, and mixed drinks, or alone as an aperitif.

To make:
 4 cups *Aronia* berries, fresh or frozen, chopped coarsely
 Vodka, highest proof possible
 Flavoring (limit to one or two): lemongrass, cardamom seeds, vanilla beans, mint, citrus peel, grated fresh ginger

Place the chopped *Aronia* berries in a 1-quart canning jar with the flavoring agent of your choice. Fill the jar with vodka, leaving a 1-inch air space at the top. Close with a plastic lid or cover with plastic wrap and a canning lid ring. The mixture will need to be shaken daily for two months. It helps to write the completion date on a piece of tape adhered to the jar.

When two months have passed, it is time to strain the bitters. Line a mesh strainer with three layers of cheesecloth and pour the mixture into the strainer with a collection container underneath. After allowing the mixture to strain, press the berries gently with the back of a wooden spoon to press out remaining liquid. The liquid can then be bottled. Since the mixture contains vodka, no refrigeration is necessary. After removing the flavoring agent, the remaining berries can be frozen in small amounts to be used in meat or dessert sauce recipes.

Other Alcoholic Drinks

Aronia appeals to vintners as a colorant and a valued ingredient for wine. Several vineyards in the Midwest are making wine with *Aronia* as a blend with grapes or as a single-berry wine. The same is to be said for craft beer artisans. The next step is to take *Aronia* into the mixed-drink realm. The berry releases a pleasant and unique flavor when combined with alcohol. To your health!

Ar-Mar-Tini—Serves I
½ ounce cointreau
Splash of vanilla extract
3 ounces vodka
6 drops of *Aronia* extract or I teaspoon *Aronia* juice

Combine all ingredients. Shake over ice. Strain and serve.

Berry Vodka—Serves I
I ounce vodka
½ ounce Triple Sec
½ ounce lime juice, freshly squeezed
I tablespoon *Aronia* juice
I twist of lemon peel

Place all ingredients in a shaker; add ½ cup chipped ice and shake until blended. Pour into a glass and garnish with the lemon peel twist.

Champagne *Aronia* Style
Sugar cubes—one per drink
Aronia juice
Champagne

Soak the sugar cubes in the juice until each cube has absorbed the juice. Place a sugar cube in the bottom of each flute and fill with the champagne. The *Aronia* creates rose-colored champagne.

Bacardi-onia—Serves 1
2 ounces rum
½ lime, juiced
½ orange, juiced
1 teaspoon sugar or honey
1 tablespoon *Aronia* juice

Combine all ingredients. Shake over ice. Strain and serve.

Aronia Wine Slush—Serves 4
If you are fortunate enough to have a source for *Aronia* wine or you make your own, make this refreshing slush to sip on a warm summer day.

¾ cup berry blend or apple juice without added sugar
½ cup sugar
1½ cups *Aronia* wine

Make simple syrup with the juice and sugar by combining them in a saucepan and cooking over low heat until the sugar dissolves. Remove from the heat and cool slightly. Add the wine and stir until blended. Chill in the refrigerator, then pour into a freezer-proof container with a lid. Put in the freezer and remove every 20–30 minutes to stir. Since this mixture contains alcohol, it may take up to 12 hours to set. Serve with a sprig of mint.

Jams and Jellies

Most people who are ardent *Aronia* consumers choose to eat the berry in the simplest forms, raw or juiced, for the ultimate health benefit. But there is a place for jam and jelly and other sweetened products. These items provide a gentle introduction to the taste of the berry.

Certain conditions make a fruit ideal for jam and jelly. The pH of a fruit should be acidic or below 3.5 to eliminate the need to add an acidulant such as citric acid. An acidulant is a food with a low pH such as vinegar or citric acid. Further examples of acidulants are indicted in the glossary section. *Aronia* usually tests at 3.4 or 3.5, thus meeting this condition. Another critical component for jam and jelly is the pectin level of the fruit. In simple terms, pectin is the substance that allows the jelly liquid to form a mass. The pectin test involves combining 1 tablespoon of rubbing alcohol with 1 teaspoon of extracted juice. After sitting for 2 minutes, a good solid mass will form if there is enough natural pectin. The test with the *Aronia* juice does not produce a mass, indicating the need to add commercial pectin to the jam and jelly mixture.

Sugar amounts vary from recipe to recipe, and while it is tempting to reduce the amount of sugar, this can greatly affect the setting of the jam/jelly. Honey can be used as a substitute for up to 2 cups of the sugar in the recipe. There are also granulated sugar substitutes which can be used. The freezer jam/jelly does not involve heat, which makes it more ideal for sugar modification. Pectin is available in a sugar-free powder. Use of this pectin form is best with cooked recipes versus the freezer variety.

Aronia in jam and/or jelly is best when combined with other fruits or fruit juices for a more pleasing flavor. The berries or juice used for jam and jelly can be fresh or frozen, making it possible to have a wonderful batch of jam or jelly simmering on a cold, wintery day. *Aronia* jam/jelly can be made using methods for the freezer or water bath canning.

Freezer Method for Jam: This method does not require any special equipment. Containers can be either freezer-proof plastics or glass jars with freezer-proof lids. It is important to have containers that will be moisture and vapor proof. All containers should be clean and sanitized, since this method does not have a bacteria-destroying heat process. If you are uncertain about the container's sanitation, merely prepare a 10 percent bleach solution (1 part bleach with 9 parts water). Dip the container and lid in the solution, rinse in clear water, and let air dry. The following are important steps to remember:

- Use dry pectin labeled as instant or for freezer jam, and follow the general directions.
- If you are using berries from the freezer, let them reach room temperature before proceeding.
- After making the jam, pour the batch into the containers, leaving at least ½ inch of headspace for expansion.
- Place the containers in the refrigerator for 24 hours to allow the jam to set before putting it in the freezer.
- Always label the jam with the ingredients, date, and cook's name.

Freezer Method for Jelly: There are numerous online recipes for nonprocessed freezer jellies. Some use powdered pectin and some liquid pectin. Since the *Aronia* juice is too astringent alone, it is recommended that one-third to one-half of the prepared juice come from another berry source. Bottled juices make an easy addition, and the wide variety of options allows for creativity. Sanitization methods mentioned in the jam section should be observed for freezer jelly as well. Freezer *Aronia* jelly may take a week to set up in the refrigerator and never becomes an extremely firm jelly.

Hot Water Bath Processing Method for Jam and Jelly:

Equipment: The novice cook is sometimes intimidated by the thought of "canning." Yet with modern day appliances and equipment, canning is as easy as making a batch of brownies. Jam and jelly batches are small enough that special equipment is usually not needed. The jars can fit easily into a large, deep stock pot. The pot needs to be deep enough to allow the jars to be completely immersed in water with about an inch of water on top. Since the water will be boiling, an additional 2 or 3 inches of air space above is recommended so the water doesn't boil over. It helps to have a rack that can go in the bottom of the pan to allow boiling water space around the entire jar. Some cooks use a round cake cooling rack in the bottom. If you are going to process other foods in a hot water bath, a boiling water canner is a good investment. Boiling water canners are inexpensive and easy to find in local stores. They have a rack which is helpful in lowering/raising the jars and helps to keep the jars spaced correctly while processing.

Containers: Glass jars specified for canning must be used. Jars for jelly and jam come in a variety of shapes and patterns, making them attractive for gifts. Normally a 6-ounce glass (¾ cup) is a nice size for gift giving. If, however, the jelly is going to be for peanut butter and jelly sandwiches all week, an 8-ounce jar might be better. Canning jars have a threaded neck to accommodate the screw band. The screw band fits over a flat metal lid. To prepare the canning jars, lids, and rings for processing, they must be clean and warm. A dishwasher is a good place to wash and dry the jars, and, if timed correctly, they will be hot when you are ready to use them. The screw bands and flat lids should be sterilized in boiling water for 5–10 minutes. They can be removed from the boiling water with a pair of tongs or a canning wand that has a magnet at the end for easy pickup. When getting ready to process the jam/jelly, the mixture and containers should be hot and the water in the stock pot or canner boiling.

Processing: Ladle the jam/jelly into the jar, leaving ¼-inch headspace. Wipe the jar rim and center the flat lid on the jar. Place the ring on the jar and screw the ring down tight. Place the jars in the canner. If there is not enough water to cover, add boiling water heated in the microwave or a saucepan. It is a good idea to have this water ready to use if needed. Put a lid on the pot, return the water to a boil, and simmer for 10 minutes with the lid on. A gentle boil is better than a hard boil, which may disturb the jars and jostle them around. When the time has expired, remove the lid and take the canner off the heat source, but let the jars remain in the water for another 5 minutes before removing to a cooling rack on the counter. Special jar tongs make this step much easier and are a good investment. Let the jars cool on the counter without being disturbed. As the vacuum seal is created, the lids will pop. To confirm all jars are sealed, tap the lids with your finger. A solid sound will be heard with those that have sealed. If they have not sealed, they will sound hollow when tapped and the lid will not be firm. Place the jars that have not been sealed in the refrigerator for use within 3 weeks.

Additional uses for jam/jelly:

- Thin slightly with apple juice to make syrup. Use the syrup on pancakes, waffles, ice cream, or sliced peaches and pears.
- Thin with a small amount of red wine or apple juice and use as meat glaze.
- Put a dollop on cottage cheese.
- Spread a thin glaze on cake layers before frosting.
- Add a spoonful to smoothies for sweetening.
- Use in thumbprint cookies
- Spread on crepes, then add a scoop of vanilla ice cream and roll up. Top with a chocolate sauce and voila!

Basic *Aronia* Freezer Jam—Makes 3 cups
2½ cups blueberries
1½ cups *Aronia* berries
1 package (1.59 ounces) freezer jam pectin
1½ cups sugar
Clean freezer containers

Both berries should be free of stems and well rinsed. If the berries are frozen, allow them to reach room temperature before proceeding. Combine both berries in a food processor and pulse until coarse. If using a small processor, it is best to chop the berries in two batches. Meanwhile mix the powdered pectin with the sugar in a large bowl. Stir to blend and eliminate chunks. Add the fruit mixture and stir until combined. Let the jam rest for 30 minutes. Ladle the jam into the prepared containers, leaving ½- to ¾-inch headspace for expansion. Wipe the container rims and place the lids on the containers. Refrigerate for 24 hours before moving to the freezer. Remove the jam from the freezer and thaw in the refrigerator before use. Since there are no preservatives, the jam should be stored in the refrigerator after opening.

Basic *Aronia* Freezer Jelly—Makes 5 cups
1 cup *Aronia* juice
1 cup apple or berry blend juice

4 cups sugar
2 tablespoons water
3 ounces liquid pectin

Combine the juices and stir. Add the sugar and blend until sugar dissolves. Allow the solution to rest for 10 minutes. Combine the water and liquid pectin in a small bowl. Add to the juice and sugar mixture and stir until the sugar has dissolved completely. Pour into the prepared containers, leaving ½- to ¾-inch headspace. Cover and let rest on the counter for 24 hours before placing in the freezer.

Basic *Aronia* Cooked Jelly—Makes 7 cups
2 cups *Aronia* juice
1½ cups apple juice, unsweetened
½ cup lemon juice, freshly squeezed
1 package (3 ounces) liquid pectin
6 cups sugar

Sterilize jars, lids, and rings, and keep heated. Pour the *Aronia* and apple juices into a large nonreactive pan. Stir in the lemon juice and one packet of liquid pectin. Bring this mixture to a boil, stirring constantly. Add the sugar and continue to stir until it has completed a full rolling boil for 2 minutes. Remove from heat; skim off the foam with a metal spoon. Pour the jelly into the hot jars, seal, and process in the water bath.

Cherry-Berry Cooked Jam—Makes 6 cups
3 cups sour cherries, pitted
1 cup *Aronia* berries
1 box (1.75 ounces) fruit pectin
½ teaspoon butter
4¾ cups sugar

Use clean fresh or frozen cherries and *Aronia* berries with stems and pits removed. If the berries are frozen, allow them to defrost. Combine the two fruits in a bowl and then divide into three batches to chop in a food processor. Use the pulse setting and crush to a coarse mixture. This step can be completed manually with a potato masher, too. Pour the fruit mixture into a 4-quart non-reactive saucepan.

Add the fruit pectin to the fruit mixture with the butter. Bring the fruit and pectin mixture to a full boil on high heat while stirring constantly. Quickly add the sugar and let the mixture return to a full boil and continue to boil for another minute while stirring. Remove from the heat and use a metal spoon to skim off any foam. The butter helps to reduce the foam amount.

Ladle or pour the jam into the hot jars and process according to general canning directions.

Spiced-Up Jelly—Makes 3 cups
This jelly is great with cream cheese on crackers or as a glaze for meats or fish.

¾ cup minced bell peppers
½ jalapeno pepper (seeds removed), diced
½ cup *Aronia* berries, coarsely chopped
2 garlic cloves, minced
1½ cups apple cider vinegar
1 cup *Aronia* juice
½ teaspoon butter
5 cups sugar
3 ounces liquid pectin

Combine the first 4 ingredients with the apple cider vinegar in a nonreactive pan. Stir to mix and place on the range over high heat. Stir constantly and bring the mixture to a boil. Allow the mixture to boil for 1 minute, then remove from the heat. Let the mixture rest while covered for 30 minutes to create an infusion in the vinegar. Strain the vinegar into a liquid measuring cup. Add enough water to the vinegar to make 1½ cups. Rinse out the nonreactive pan and pour the vinegar back in. Add the *Aronia* juice, butter, and sugar and bring the mixture to a boil over medium-high heat, stirring constantly to help dissolve the sugar. Lower the heat and continue to simmer for another minute. Stir in the pectin and bring to a hard boil while stirring. Let the mixture boil for 1 minute before removing the pan from the heat. Skim off any foam with a metal spoon and process into jars according to general directions.

What's for Dinner?

The most nutritious use of *Aronia* is to use little or no heat. *Aronia* can still be used with meats and cooked vegetables in sauces which aren't cooked. Some of the recipes in this section do allow minimal exposure to heat, while some do not. For those requiring heat, remember to use slow cooking methods at a lower temperature when possible.

Meat Glaze—Makes 1½ cups
2 tablespoons dry sherry
1 tablespoon soy sauce
¼ cup *Aronia* berries, dehydrated and chopped
1 cup *Aronia* jelly(recipe in Jams and Jellies chapter)

Combine all ingredients in a saucepan and heat over low heat until the jelly melts. Let the mixture continue to cook for an additional 2 minutes. This sauce is wonderful on grilled pork, chicken, and even grilled portobello mushrooms.

Barbecue Sauce—Makes about 3 ½ cups
2 cups tomato sauce
1 cup *Aronia* juice
¼ cup pure maple syrup
¼ cup *Aronia* vinegar (recipe in Salsa, Syrup…chapter)
2 tablespoons candied ginger, minced
2 tablespoons chili powder
2 tablespoons Worcestershire sauce
1 shallot, minced
1 garlic clove, minced
2 teaspoons black pepper
1 teaspoon liquid hot pepper sauce

Combine all ingredients in a 4-quart nonreactive saucepan. Stir until ingredients are well-combined. Simmer for 20 minutes over medium-high heat, stirring frequently. Simmer for an additional 10–15 minutes. The sauce will begin to thicken and may burn if it is not stirred often.

The sauce can be spread on roasted/grilled pork, beef, or chicken during the last 20 minutes. Or, add to shredded meat to create a pulled sandwich filling.

Poultry Sauce—Makes 2 ½ cups
2 tablespoons olive oil
2 tablespoons all-purpose flour
½ cup *Aronia* juice
1 ½ cups apple juice
½ cup *Aronia* berries, chopped coarsely
2 tablespoons crystallized ginger, finely chopped

Heat the olive oil in a pan on medium-low heat. Add the flour and stir to make a paste (roux). Let the roux bubble for a minute while stirring, but avoid burning. Slowly add the combined juices while stirring to prevent lumps. A wire whisk may help for this step. Continue to cook over the heat while stirring until the sauce thickens. Add the berries and ginger and stir. Serve hot with grilled or roasted chicken or turkey.

Stuffed Pork Chops—Serves 4
1 Granny Smith apple, peeled, cored, and chopped
½ cup prunes, chopped
½ cup *Aronia* berries
1 teaspoon lemon peel, freshly grated
4 pork chops, thick cut and boneless
Salt and pepper to taste
1 cup apple juice
1 tablespoon cornstarch dissolved in 2 tablespoons cold water
1 tablespoon *Aronia* juice

Combine apple, prunes, berries, and lemon peel. Cut a pocket in each chop by slicing midway along one outer edge. Divide the filling into four equal portions and stuff into each pork chop cavity. Salt and pepper each side of the chops. Place in an oven-proof pan and bake at 375°F for 1¼ hour or until the meat thermometer reaches 170°F.

Begin the sauce when there is about 20 minutes remaining on the roasting time. Heat the apple juice in a small pan over medium-high heat. When the juice begins to boil, reduce the temperature to a simmer. Mix the cornstarch mixture and *Aronia* juice. Add to the simmering apple juice, stirring constantly until the sauce thickens. Serve the sauce warm on top of the pork chops.

Chicken Breasts with A/B Sauce—Serves 4
Chicken:
4 small chicken breast halves, boned and skinned
Salt and pepper to taste
2 teaspoons olive oil
Sauce:
1 cup blueberries
1 cup *Aronia* berries, fresh or frozen
2 tablespoons *Aronia* infused vinegar (recipe in Salsa, Syrup…chapter)
1 tablespoon water
1 tablespoon corn syrup
1 teaspoon orange rind

Chicken Breasts: Place the breasts between two pieces of wax paper and flatten them slightly with either a rolling pin or the side of a dredger. Season lightly with salt and pepper on both sides. Heat the olive oil in a skillet on medium-high heat. Sauté the chicken breasts in the hot oil for approximately 5 minutes on each side until they begin to brown. Reduce the heat to low and continue until they are cooked thoroughly, turning as needed.

Sauce: Combine the first six ingredients in a nonreactive pan. Bring to a boil, then reduce the heat and simmer for 10 minutes or until the skins on the *Aronia* berries and blueberries have cracked and the berries have softened. Remove from the burner and pour into a serving bowl or pitcher to serve with the chicken. Or, the chicken breasts can be arranged on a platter with the sauce poured over before serving. The sauce can be served hot or cold.

A Bit of Health Soup—Serves 5 or 6

1 pound of extra-lean ground beef or ground turkey
1 onion, chopped
2 (14½-ounce) cans stewed tomatoes, low sodium
2 cups tomato juice
1 cup *Aronia* berries
1 (15¼-ounce) can corn, drained
Pesto, optional

Sauté the meat and onions in a nonstick skillet until browned. Combine all ingredients except the pesto in a slow cooker and cook on low for 5 to 6 hours. To serve, ladle into bowls and top with a spoonful of pesto.

Gazpacho *Aronia* Style—Serves 6

1 cup tomato juice
½ cup *Aronia* berries
2 cloves garlic, minced
½ jalapeno pepper, seeded and minced
⅓ cup olive oil
2 tablespoons *Aronia* vinegar or red wine vinegar
½ teaspoon black pepper
½ teaspoon cumin
4 tomatoes, diced with skins
4 plum tomatoes, diced with skins
1 green pepper, seeded and diced
1 cucumber, peeled, seeded and diced
6 scallions, sliced crosswise, including green tops
Sour cream

Place the first eight ingredients in a blender and process until smooth. Add the remaining chopped vegetables. Chill in the refrigerator for a minimum of 12 hours to blend flavors. Serve topped with a spoonful of sour cream.

<u>Squasharoni—Serves 4</u>
1 butternut squash, skinned and cut into 1-inch cubes
2 shallots, sliced
½ cup *Aronia* berries
2 tablespoons olive oil
1 teaspoon dried rosemary, chopped, or 2 teaspoons fresh rosemary

Preheat the oven to 425°F. Place all ingredients in a plastic bag and toss to combine. The bag can be kept in the refrigerator for up to an hour to allow the flavors to blend. Spread the mixture evenly in a single layer on a baking sheet. Roast for about 30–40 minutes, turning halfway through with a metal spatula. The vegetables should be nicely browned without burning.

The *Aronia melanocarpa* shrub is adorned in the spring with beautiful white flowers and a touch of pink.

Fall brings a reddish hue to the leaves further enhancing the landscape with color.

Berries from the 'Viking' cultivar are shown on the right. On the left are berries from 'Autumn Magic.' While both offer nutritional value the 'Viking' provides more juice and flavor.

Dehydration of the *Aronia* berry allows a concentrated product which is easy to store.

Juicing the berry creates two consumable products – juice and pomace.

Aronia for breakfast can start the day in several nutritious forms.

Hand blended teas with *Aronia* are fun to make and more economical than those sold commercially. Many of the ingredients can be grown in a backyard herb garden (e.g. lemon verbena, mint, stevia).

Easy to prepare...*Aronia* jams and jellies make great gifts.

Fruit roll-ups with *Aronia* offer a healthy snack or addition to the lunch box.

Aronia juice used in cake mixes adds a unique flavor and hue.

Healthy can be fun too! Dehyrated *Aronia* bits give this popcorn mix an extra crunch.

Ready to take on the trail, pemmican is a concentrated health/energy bar.

Aronia frozen desserts accompanied with *Aronia* shortbread cookies are the perfect way to end a meal or indulge in at any time.

Enjoy easy and fun to make *Aronia* products for the bath.

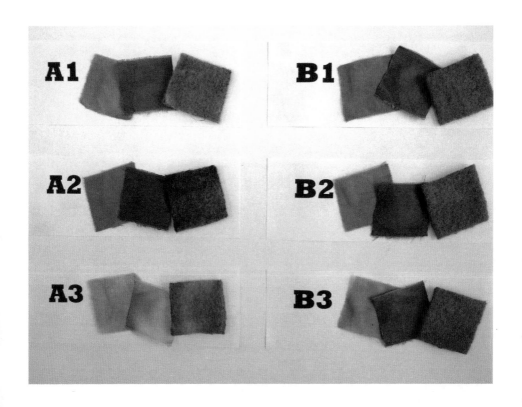

All samples have been dyed in *Aronia* juice. Colors vary depending on the technique.

Our pets can benefit from *Aronia* too.

Salsas, Sauces, Syrups, and Dressings

Aronia berries ripen at about the same time as the garden comes into full production. This is a perfect opportunity to add the berries to a favorite of many—salsa. And along with a bountiful garden come fresh garden salads, which can be glazed with *Aronia* dressings. These recipes can still be made in the middle of winter with berries from the freezer.

Dressings and Salads:

Aronia Infused Vinegar—Makes 2 cups
2 cups apple cider vinegar
⅓ cup *Aronia* berries

Pour the apple cider vinegar into an acid-proof pan. Heat until the vinegar begins to boil. If you use the microwave, this takes about 4–6 minutes on high. Coarsely chop the berries in a food processor or place in a small plastic bag and hit with a flat object. Add the berries to the hot vinegar. Leave the berries in the vinegar for at least 48 hours before pouring through a strainer into a cruet. A paper coffee filter works well to use as a filter. Keep the vinegar refrigerated. Use for salad dressings where red wine vinegar is indicated or for any dishes using apple cider vinegar. If a more intense berry-flavored vinegar is desired leave the berries in the vinegar and refrigerate without straining.

Berry Vinaigrette—Makes ½ cup
¼ cup low-saturated-fat oil, such as canola, corn, or safflower oil
2 tablespoons extra virgin olive oil
1 tablespoon *Aronia* juice
1 tablespoon *Aronia* or red wine vinegar(recipe in Salsa, Sauces…chapter)
1 tablespoon orange juice
Salt and pepper to taste

Mix all ingredients in a jar. Cover and shake vigorously until blended. Use immediately or store in the refrigerator until needed; shake again before serving.

<u>*Aronia* Dressing—Makes ⅓ cup</u>
2 tablespoons *Aronia* jelly (recipe in the Jams and Jellies chapter)
2 tablespoons *Aronia* vinegar
1½ tablespoons extra virgin olive oil
Salt and pepper to taste

Combine all ingredients in a jar. Cover and shake until well blended. Use immediately. Store any remaining dressing in the refrigerator. This is a refreshing dressing for the following spinach salad.

<u>Spinach and Fruit Salad—Serves 6</u>
6 cups spinach, washed and broken into bite-size pieces
½ small red onion, sliced into thin rings
2 navel oranges, peeled and sliced crosswise
Aronia Dressing (above)
2 tablespoons *Aronia* berry bits, dehydrated and coarsely chopped
⅓ cup pecans, chopped

Place the spinach in a large bowl. Add the sliced onions, oranges, and dressing, and toss. Sprinkle the top with the *Aronia* bits and pecans.

<u>Slaw *Aronia* Style—Serves 4</u>
Dressing:
2 tablespoons *Aronia* vinegar (recipe in Salsas, Sauces…chapter)
2 tablespoons olive oil
1 tablespoon honey or agave syrup
½ teaspoon poppy seeds
1 tablespoon plain or lemon fat-free yogurt

Salad:
1 ½ cups strawberries, stems removed and sliced
½ cup mandarin orange slices, fresh or canned (drained)

2 cups finely shredded cabbage
1 tablespoon *Aronia* bits, dehydrated

Blend all dressing ingredients in a food processor or blender until the mixture is smooth. Combine the salad ingredients in a large bowl. Add the dressing and toss to combine. Chill the slaw for at least two hours before serving. Flavors blend further if allowed to refrigerate for a day.

Appetizers and Salsa:

Chutney—Makes about 4 cups
1 cup *Aronia* berries, frozen
1 cup seedless red grapes
2 tablespoons extra virgin olive oil
½ cup shallots, minced
1 tablespoon garlic, minced
1 teaspoon cumin seeds
1 cup red bell pepper, seeded and diced
1 jalapeno pepper, seeded and minced
¼ cup golden raisins
1 tablespoon gingerroot, grated
¼ cup cider vinegar
¼ cup white grape juice
2 tablespoons light brown sugar
¼ teaspoon salt

Prepare all ingredients. Chop berries and grapes together in a food processor until chunky. Heat the olive oil in a nonstick pan on medium heat. Add shallots, garlic, and cumin seeds to hot oil and sauté until the garlic and shallots are golden but not brown, stirring constantly to prevent burning. Add the grape/*Aronia* mixture, peppers, raisins, gingerroot, and vinegar to the mixture. Simmer, covered, at a reduced temperature (medium-low) for about 15 minutes. Add grape juice and sugar and simmer for an additional 15 minutes with the lid removed to allow liquid to evaporate. Stir as needed to prevent burning. Let the mixture cool before adding the salt.

Keep the chutney refrigerated until ready to use. Or, process the chutney using a water bath canning method for 10 minutes. The chutney can be frozen for up to six months as well.

To serve: Top toasted slices of crusty bread with chevre or cream cheese and a dollop of chutney.

Salsa has replaced ketchup as the preferred condiment. There are so many possible combinations with garden vegetables and orchard fruits. Salsas are at home on a chip, scrambled eggs, sandwiches, grilled meats, and anything else one might fancy.

West of the Missouri Salsa—Makes 6 cups
1 cup *Aronia* berries, fresh or frozen
1 serrano pepper, seeded and chopped
2 jalapeno peppers, seeded and cut into pieces
1 garlic clove, minced
2 cups tomatoes, seeded and diced (juicy slicer tomatoes are better than plum)
1 yellow bell pepper, seeded and chopped
6–7 scallions, sliced thin crosswise
½ cup cucumber, peeled, seeded, and cut into ¼-inch cubes
½ teaspoon cumin
Sea salt and pepper to taste

Place the berries in a food processor with the blade attached and pulse to chop the berries until they are coarse. Add the hot peppers, garlic, and about ¼ cup tomatoes. Pulse until they are finely chopped but not pureed. In a large bowl combine the mixture with the remaining tomatoes, yellow pepper, scallions, cucumber, and cumin by tossing gently. Add sea salt and pepper to taste. If the tomatoes are not juicy enough, add the juice of 1 lime or ¼ cup tomato juice.

Salsa on the Edge—Makes 4 cups
2½ cups *Aronia* berries, frozen
1 tablespoon orange liqueur
¼ cup orange juice
1 lime, juiced

½ teaspoon cumin
2 cloves garlic, finely chopped
2 jalapeno chilies, stemmed, seeded, and finely diced
1 mango, skinned and cubed
½ cup cilantro leaves, chopped
6 scallions, sliced thin crosswise
Sea salt to taste

Place the frozen berries in a food processor with the blade attachment. Pulse until the berries are chopped coarsely.

Mix the orange liqueur, orange juice, lime juice, and cumin in a small bowl. In a larger bowl toss the chopped berries with the garlic, chilies, mango, cilantro, and scallions. Add the liquid mixture and toss to combine. Season with sea salt to taste.

The salsa should be served at room temperature, but if the salsa is not going to be used immediately, store it in the refrigerator until 15 minutes before serving. This is a nice companion to grilled chicken or fish.

Syrup:

Simple Syrup—Makes 2 cups
This is great syrup for pancakes and waffles, plus it can be poured over shaved ice for a snow cone. The sugar can be replaced with a granulated no-calorie sweetener, or use a 50/50 mix of sugar and granulated no-calorie sugar substitute.

2 cups sugar or sweetener
½ cup apple or berry juice
½ cup *Aronia* juice

Mix all ingredients in a 2-quart saucepan. Bring the mixture to a boil over medium-high heat while stirring. Allow the mixture to continue to boil for an additional minute before removing from the heat. A silicone scraper is useful to stir since it can keep the bottom from burning and it tolerates high heat. When the syrup has cooled, pour it into a container and store in the refrigerator.

<u>Rhubarb and *Aronia* Berry Sauce</u>—Makes 2 cups
½ cup fresh or frozen *Aronia* berries
1 ¼ cups fresh or frozen rhubarb, leaves removed and cut into 1-inch pieces
¾ cup apple juice or water
½ cup granulated sugar
1 teaspoon cornstarch
1 tablespoon cold water

Place the berries and rhubarb in a large pan. Add the apple juice/water and bring the mixture to a boil over medium-high heat. Stir occasionally. Once the mixture has reached the boil stage lower the temperature to medium-low and simmer for 10 minutes. Add the sugar and continue to stir until the sugar has dissolved completely. Meanwhile combine the cornstarch and tablespoon of water in a small dish. Add to the rhubarb and berry mixture stirring constantly to avoid lumps forming. Continue to cook over low heat while stirring until the mixture has thickened. Remove from the heat and allow to cool. The sauce can be used immediately or stored in the refrigerator in an airtight container. This sauce is wonderful on pancakes or waffles and makes an interesting addition to grilled chicken or pork.

Snacks and Desserts

Snacks and desserts can be healthier versions of those from years past which were high in sugars, fats, and processed grains. Now they are prepared as part of a meal's total package in meeting food pyramid guidelines. The inclusion of *Aronia* in the recipes in this section provides an additional way to ease those new to the berry into adding the taste to their palate choices while enhancing the health benefits.

Aronia Jellies—Makes twenty-one 1-inch cubes
4 tablespoons (2 packets) unflavored gelatin
1 cup *Aronia* juice
1 cup apple juice, unsweetened
1 tablespoon honey or agave syrup

Spray a 3x7-inch loaf pan with a mist of water. Soften the gelatin in the *Aronia* juice for 5 minutes, stirring occasionally. Heat the apple juice and sweetener over medium-low heat in a small saucepan or in the microwave. Stir to blend the juice and sweetener, then add to the softened gelatin. Pour into the loaf pan and place in the refrigerator for a minimum of 3 hours until the jelly is set.

To serve, run a knife or the edge of a metal spatula along the outside of the pan to loosen the mixture. Cut across the length and the width to make approximately 1-inch squares. Invert the pan onto wax paper to remove the jellies from the pan. Since the jellies are somewhat sticky, they can be dusted lightly with castor (superfine) sugar.

Aroni-Rollups—Makes 8 to 10 servings
2 cups applesauce, unsweetened
1 cup *Aronia* berries, fresh or frozen
2 tablespoons honey or agave syrup

Place all ingredients in a food processor and blend until smooth. Pour the mixture onto food dehydrator liner sheets in an even thickness between ⅓ and ¼ inch. A spatula or dough scraper is useful to spread the mixture evenly. Use two or more trays for the mixture. For dehydrators with a temperature regulator, set it to 135°F. The dehydrating time will take approximately 4 hours. For dehydrators without a temperature regulator, it may take up to eight hours or more. The fruit leather is dry when it peels easily off the sheet but is not brittle. It is possible to turn the fruit sheet over during drying to finish the opposite side, but it is not necessary. When the drying is finished, remove the fruit sheet to a cutting board and cut into strips using a pizza cutter. They can be stored as strips or rolled up.

There are applesauce blends which make an interesting roll-up with the *Aronia*. An especially tasty one can be made with pomegranate applesauce.

<u>Crunchy Popcorn—Makes 16 cups</u>
12 cups popped corn, unsalted
1 cup peanuts, dry roasted
½ cup pumpkin seeds, shelled
½ cup *Aronia* bits
1 cup M&Ms plain candy
1⅓ cups brown sugar, firmly packed
1 cup butter, unsalted
½ cup light corn syrup
½ teaspoon cream of tartar
½ teaspoon baking soda
½ teaspoon butter flavoring or vanilla extract

Combine the popcorn, peanuts, pumpkin seeds, *Aronia* bits, and M&Ms in a large bowl. Toss to combine.

Place the brown sugar, butter, corn syrup, and cream of tartar in a heavy saucepan with at least four times the volume of the ingredients. Stir gently until the sugar dissolves. Discontinue stirring and bring the mixture to a boil on medium heat. Continue the boil until a candy thermometer reads 300°F. Remove the pan from the heat and add the baking soda and flavoring. The mixture will become foamy, but it is important to pour it over the popped corn immediately. With two wooden spoons or silicone spatulas, toss the popped corn mixture with the caramel mixture to coat evenly. Allow to cool completely before breaking into chunks.

<u>Baked Apple-ronia—Serves 6</u>
6 apples, Jonathan or another baking apple
⅓ cup walnut pieces
⅓ cup *Aronia* berries
1 tablespoon brown sugar, packed
1 teaspoon cinnamon

Preheat the oven to 375°F. After coring the apples, remove about one quarter of the apple peel from the stem down. Place the walnut pieces, *Aronia* berries, brown sugar, and cinnamon in a food processor and pulse until the walnuts and berries are finely chopped. Fill the bottoms of the cored apples before placing them in a shallow baking pan. Complete filling the apples on the top side. Cover with foil and bake in the oven for 45 minutes until the apples are fork tender. Serve hot with a spoonful of vanilla ice cream.

<u>Crackers—Serves 8 to 10</u>
These crackers will become a favorite for people who lean toward raw-food diets. They are extremely high in protein and are cholesterol free.

½ cup *Aronia* juice
5½ cups water, purified
4 cups flaxseeds, golden are preferable
½ cup light soy sauce
½ cup *Aronia* berries, dehydrated and finely chopped
½ cup parsley, dried and minced

Mix the *Aronia* juice with the purified water and blend with the flaxseeds in a large glass bowl. Allow to sit for 6 hours until the flaxseeds have become gelatin-like. Add the soy sauce, dehydrated *Aronia* bits, and parsley. Mix well. Pour the mixture onto the dehydrator film trays and spread into a thin and even layer. Dry in the dehydrator at 105°F for up to 5 hours. Loosen the cracker with a spatula and flip the cracker over to dry for an additional 5 hours. The cracker should be completely dry. Remove from the dehydrator and break into pieces, or put the cracker on a cutting board and cut into portions with a pizza rotary cutter.

These crackers are sturdy enough for dipping salsa or hummus.

Dandy Candy Bites—Makes 18 to 24 candies
1 cup dark chocolate chips
1 cup flaked or shredded coconut
½ cup *Aronia* berries, dehydrated and coarsely chopped

Melt the chocolate chips in a double boiler over low heat. The microwave can be used, but set the time for 2 minutes at defrost and stir every 2 minutes. If the chocolate overcooks, it will become extremely hard. Add the coconut and *Aronia* bits to the melted chocolate and stir until combined. Work quickly and drop the mixture by tablespoonfuls onto parchment or waxed paper. Allow to cool completely. Store in an airtight container in a cool place.

Almost Red Velvet Cake—Serves 8 to 10
1 box cake mix (18.25 ounces), chocolate or devil's food
1 cup *Aronia* juice
⅓ cup water
½ cup vegetable oil
3 eggs, large

Prepare the cake according to the directions, substituting the *Aronia* juice for a portion of the water. Bake as either a layer cake or sheet cake. Before putting the pan(s) in the oven, tap the pan(s) on a counter to release the large air bubbles. If you have *Aronia* jelly, thin a small amount to use as a glaze on the top before frosting with a creamy white frosting.

Berry Crumble—Serves 6 to 8
2 cups blueberries
1 cup *Aronia* berries
1 tablespoon sugar or honey
1 tablespoon lemon juice, freshly squeezed
¼ cup flour

¼ cup rolled oats, regular or quick
¼ cup brown sugar, firmly packed
½ teaspoon cinnamon
¼ teaspoon allspice
2 tablespoons pecans, chopped
3 tablespoons butter, unsalted, softened
Vanilla ice cream or frozen yogurt

Preheat the oven to 375°F. Lightly coat the inside of an 8x8-inch baking pan with butter or a baking pan spray. Toss the berries with the sugar and lemon juice in a medium-size bowl. Spread in the baking dish and bake for 15 minutes while covered with foil. While the berries are baking, combine the flour, oats, sugar, spices, and nuts in a medium-size bowl. Add the softened butter and mix as you would pastry, using two knives, a pastry blender, or your fingers to create a crumbly mixture. Remove the berries from the oven and stir. Sprinkle the topping over the berries and return the mixture to the oven to bake, uncovered, for an additional 20 minutes. Let the crumble cool slightly before serving with your choice of ice cream or frozen yogurt.

<u>A Berry Cherry Pie—Serves 6-8</u>
1½ cups tart cherries, fresh or frozen and pitted
1 cup *Aronia* berries, fresh or frozen
3 tablespoons tapioca, quick cooking
2 cups sugar
Pie crust dough for a 9-inch double crust pie

Toss all ingredients except pie crust in a bowl and set aside while preparing the crust. Roll out half the crust dough to a thin ⅓ inch and gently place in a 9-inch pie pan. Spread the cherry/berry mixture over the bottom crust. Roll the second half of the pie crust dough for a double crust pie, or cut into lattice strips. Prior to placing the top crust or lattice strips, moisten the top edge of the crust lightly with water. Place the top crust or lattice strips in place, and crimp the edges of the bottom crust and top crust or strips together.

Bake in a 425°F oven for 15 minutes. Reduce the heat to 350°F and continue baking for another 40–45 minutes or until the crust is golden brown. If the edge is turning brown quickly, put a strip of foil around the edge to prevent burning.

Berryly Apple Pie—Serves 6-8
1 cup *Aronia* berries, dehydrated and coarsely chopped
½ cup apple brandy
1¾ pounds Jonathan apples or other baking apples (6–7 medium or 4 large)
½ teaspoon vanilla extract
⅓ cup packed brown sugar
Pie crust dough for a 9-inch double crust pie
4 tablespoons butter, unsalted, cut into small pieces

Combine the *Aronia* berries and brandy in a bowl. Set aside for 30–40 minutes to allow the berries to rehydrate. While the berries are soaking peel and core the apples then slice lengthwise into ¼ inch pieces. When the berries are plump, place them in a strainer to drain off the excess brandy. The brandy can be saved in another container to be used in a sauce recipe or as an ice cream topping. Combine the drained berries with the apple slices and toss with the vanilla extract. Add the brown sugar and gently toss all to combine. Roll out half of the pie pastry dough and line a 9-inch pie pan. Pour the apple/berry mixture into the pie pan and place the dots of butter around the filling before covering with the top crust. Trim and crimp the edges of the pie and make several slices in the top crust for steam release.

Bake in a preheated 425°F oven until the crust is golden brown, approximately 50–60 minutes.

Aronia Glazed Strawberry Pie—Serves 6-8
3 cups fresh strawberries
1 cup *Aronia* berries, fresh or frozen
1 cup granulated sugar
3 tablespoons cornstarch
¾ cup apple juice
Baked 9-inch baked pie crust, pastry or graham cracker
Whipped cream

Slice lengthwise 2 cups of strawberries. Arrange the strawberries in the bottom of the pie crust. Puree the remaining cup of strawberries with the *Aronia* berries in a food processor until the berries are finely chopped. Combine the chopped berries with the sugar in a saucepan. Place over medium heat and bring the mixture to a boil. Stir as needed to prevent scorching on the bottom of the pan.

In a small bowl combine the cornstarch with the apple juice. Mix until the cornstarch is dissolved. Add the cornstarch/juice mixture to the berry/sugar mixture slowly. Reduce the heat to medium-low to maintain a low simmer. Continue to cook for another 10 minutes or until the mixture has thickened, stirring constantly. Pour the glaze over the berries in the pie crust. Refrigerate for 4-6 hours to chill before serving. Serve each piece of pie with a spoonful of whipped cream.

Tea Bread—Serves 8-10
1 cup unbleached all-purpose flour
1 cup white whole-wheat flour
1 teaspoon salt
1½ teaspoons baking powder
½ teaspoon baking soda
1 tablespoon butter, unsalted, softened
1 cup sugar
1 large egg
¾ cup apple juice
1 cup *Aronia* berries, dehydrated and chopped
1 cup pecans, chopped

Preheat oven to 350°F. Lightly grease a 9x5-inch loaf pan. Sift together both types of flour, salt, baking powder, and baking soda into a large bowl. Cream butter and sugar in a large bowl until sugar is dissolved. Add the egg and continue blending until well mixed. Add dry ingredients alternating with apple juice and blend until moist. Do not overmix. Gently fold in *Aronia* berries and chopped pecans. Pour into the prepared pan and gently tap the bottom of the pan on a hard surface to release any large air bubbles. Bake for 50–55 minutes or until an inserted toothpick is clean when removed.

<u>*Aronia* Shortbread—Makes 3 dozen cookies</u>
¾ cup sugar
I cup butter, unsalted, at room temperature
I teaspoon vanilla extract
4 tablespoons milk, nonfat or I percent
2½ cups all-purpose flour
½ teaspoon salt
½ cup macadamia nuts, chopped
½ cup *Aronia* berries, dehydrated and coarsely chopped
Optional: Chocolate almond bark

Cream the sugar and butter in a bowl using an electric mixer until the mixture is fluffy and light in color, about 2 minutes. Add the vanilla and milk and continue mixing until all ingredients are combined. Add the remaining ingredients and stir with a wooden spoon until the mixture is well blended.

Turn the dough onto a piece of wax paper and divide into two equal pieces. Shape each piece into an 8-inch-long log which is about 2 inches in diameter. Wrap both logs firmly with plastic wrap and place in the refrigerator to chill until they are firm (about 90 minutes). Preheat the oven to 375°F. Using a sharp knife or dental floss, slice the logs into ½-inch-thick pieces. If using dental floss—make sure it is not a flavored variety—put the floss underneath the log and pull the floss up and around to create slices. Place the slices on parchment-paper-lined baking sheets about I inch apart. Gently flatten the cookies with the palm of your hand. Bake for 14–15 minutes until the edges are golden brown. If you are using a convection oven, you do not need to rotate the trays, but if using a conventional oven, it helps to rotate the trays halfway through the baking. Transfer baked cookies to a cooling rack.

For an extra decorative touch dip one edge of the cooled cookie in melted chocolate almond bark. Place on a piece of waxed paper to allow the almond bark to harden.

<u>*Aronia*-Filled Tea Cakes—Makes 18 cakes</u>
Filling:
¼ cup apple juice, unsweetened
¼ cup sugar

¾ cup *Aronia* berries, fresh or frozen, chopped coarsely

¼ cup apricots (dried), chopped

3 tablespoons pecans, finely chopped1 tablespoon all-purpose flour

Cookie Dough:

¾ cup butter, unsalted, softened

1¼ cups sugar

2 large eggs, slightly beaten

1 teaspoon vanilla extract

½ cup milk or soy milk

3¼ cups all-purpose flour

1½ teaspoons baking powder

1 teaspoon baking soda

2 teaspoons cream of tartar

Topping:

1 egg white

1 tablespoon water

Sugar sprinkles

To make the filling, heat the apple juice and sugar in a small saucepan or microwave and stir to dissolve the sugar. Add the *Aronia* berries to the sugar syrup and let sit off the heat until cool. Add the apricots and pecans to the cooled mixture and stir to blend all ingredients. Sprinkle with the tablespoon of flour and mix in. Set aside while making the cookie dough.

To make the dough, in a large mixing bowl cream together the butter and sugar. Beat in the eggs and mix until mixture lightens in color. Add the vanilla and milk and mix until all ingredients are blended. On a piece of waxed paper or in another mixing bowl, combine the flour, baking powder, baking soda and cream of tartar and stir with a wire whisk or fork to blend. Or, the dry ingredients can be sifted together to blend. Add the dry ingredients to the creamed butter/sugar mixture and mix by hand with a wooden spoon or spatula. Divide the dough into two halves and wrap each half in waxed paper or plastic wrap. Place in the refrigerator to chill for about 30 minutes.

Preheat the oven to 350°F. Before rolling out the dough, sprinkle the area with flour. Remove one of the dough halves and roll out to about ¼-inch thickness. The dough is sticky, but a light dusting on top, with flour and waxed paper on top to be between the dough and the rolling pin, eases the process. Use a cookie cutter or glass to cut out 2½-inch circles. Keep the bottom of the cutter coated with flour as you work to assist in easy removal of the circles. Place the cutouts on a cookie sheet which has been greased lightly or lined with parchment paper. These tea cakes double in size, so keep them at least 2–3 inches apart. Repeat this process with the second half of the dough to use as the tops.

Before using the filling, pour off excess fluid from the mixture. Then place a tablespoon of the filling in the center of half of the circles. Cover with the top circle and gently press around the base to join the two halves.

Mix the egg white with the water and brush over the tops of the tea cakes before sprinkling with the sugar. Place in the oven and bake for around 15 minutes or until the tops become a golden color. Allow to cool slightly on the cookie sheet before removing them with a metal spatula to the cooling rack.

Easy No-Bake Cookies—Makes 18 to 24 cookies

½ cup butter, unsalted

⅔ cup sugar

3 tablespoons unsweetened cocoa powder

2 tablespoons brewed coffee

½ teaspoon vanilla extract

1½ cups quick-cooking rolled oats, processed in the food processor to create a coarse flour

½ cup *Aronia* berries, dehydrated and coarsely chopped

⅓ cup pecans, chopped

Confectioners' sugar

6 ounces almond bark, chocolate flavored

Cream together the first five ingredients until fluffy. Add the oats, *Aronia* berries, and pecans and mix by hand until well blended. Form the mixture into 1-inch balls and roll in the confectioners' sugar. Place on wax paper, cover with foil, and allow to set in the refrigerator for 24 hours. The mixture will be very moist, but the oatmeal will absorb the moisture during the resting period in the refrigerator. When the cookies are set, melt the almond bark in a double boiler on low heat or in the microwave at 50 percent power. If using the microwave, heat in 2-minute increments and stir in between until the almond bark is melted and smooth. Dribble the melted bark over the tops of the cookies to coat the top.

<u>Chewy Chunky Cookies—Makes about 6 dozen cookies</u>
1 cup butter, unsalted, softened
¾ cup light brown sugar, packed
¾ cup sugar
2 eggs
2 teaspoons vanilla extract
1¼ cups all-purpose flour
1 teaspoon baking powder
1 teaspoon salt
2½ cups rolled oats, regular
2 ounces macadamia nuts, chopped
2 cups white chocolate chips (12ounces)
1 cup *Aronia* berries, dehydrated and chopped

Preheat the oven to 350°F. In a large mixing bowl, cream the butter with the sugars until fluffy. Add the eggs one at a time and beat after each addition. Add the vanilla and stir to mix. In a separate bowl or on a piece of waxed paper, sift together the flour, baking powder, and salt. In a bowl or bag, place the oats, nuts, chocolate chips, and berries, and shake until well mixed. Stir the flour mixture into the sugar/butter mixture and mix with a wooden spoon until well blended. Add the oat mixture and fold into the dough until the ingredients are well dispersed.

Drop the batter by tablespoonfuls onto a cookie sheet lined with parchment paper or a silicone baking mat. Bake for 10–12 minutes until browned on top. Remove and let rest for a few minutes before transferring to a cooling rack.

<u>Healthy Fruit Drop Cookies—Makes about 5 dozen cookies</u>
2 cups dried cherries, chopped
2½ cups dried apricots, diced
1 cup *Aronia* berries, dehydrated and coarsely chopped
1½ cups raisins or dates, chopped
1½ cups apples (dried), diced

1 cup pecans, chopped
1¾ cups all-purpose flour
½ cup butter, unsalted, at room temperature
1 cup dark brown sugar, packed
1 teaspoon salt
½ teaspoon baking powder
2 large eggs, lightly beaten
½ cup *Aronia* juice (apple juice can be used as a substitution)
1 teaspoon cinnamon
½ teaspoon ground allspice

Preheat the oven to 325°F. Line cookie sheets with parchment paper or grease lightly. Combine the dried fruits and nuts in a large bowl and toss with one quarter of the flour to help separate the fruit. In another bowl, mix the butter, sugar, salt, and baking powder by hand or with a mixer on low speed until blended. Add the eggs one at a time and beat after each addition until creamy.

Blend in the *Aronia* juice followed by the spices. Add the remaining 1½ cups of flour and mix until smooth. Fold in the dried fruit/nut mixture with a wooden spoon until well blended.

Drop heaping tablespoons of the cookie dough onto the cookie sheet, leaving 1½ inches between cookies. Place in the oven and bake for 21–23 minutes. Let them rest on the cookie sheet for a few minutes before transferring them to a cooling rack.

Once Upon a Time

The Native Americans in the northeastern regions of the United States and southeastern portions of Canada lived a rigorous life hunting and trapping game and fur. To provide sustenance for their long, cold winter journeys, they created a food called pemmican. This high-density, nutritious precursor to the modern-day food bar was a concentrated mixture of ground dried meat, animal fat, nuts, and berries. Among the berries native to this region was *Aronia*, which had already been recognized by the Native Americans for possessing qualities beneficial to health. When the European fur traders, mainly French, came to the new world to trap and hunt, they learned of pemmican and began to take it with them on their long journeys as well.

Modern-day diets and lifestyles are a far cry from those of our predecessors. Pemmican, however, is still a food source for wilderness campers and hikers. Since it is a high-energy food, it is eaten by sports enthusiasts when participating in such activities as cross-country skiing and canoeing. This updated version of pemmican does not include buffalo meat or lard, so the taste is not exactly as it was a few hundred years ago. But the same nutritional value exists, as well as ease of storage.

Modern-Day Pemmican—Makes about 21 blocks
3.25 ounces beef jerky (beef or turkey)
½ cup almonds, roasted and unsalted
½ cup *Aronia* pomace or dehydrated *Aronia* berries
½ teaspoon chili powder (optional, but adds a little zip)
½ cup almond butter or peanut butter, creamy and natural (without salt and sugar)
I tablespoon honey

Cut the jerky into chunks and place in a food processor with the metal blade attachment. Add the almonds and process until a coarse crumb is formed, void of large chunks. Add the remaining ingredients and pulse until the mixture begins to draw away from the side of the processor bowl. Make a ball to see how well the mixture stays together. The amount of nut butter (which is the fat replacement) can vary with the season and humidity, so you may need to add more. Meanwhile line a 3x7-inch loaf pan with plastic wrap. Press the pemmican mixture into the bottom of the pan and spread evenly. Cover and refrigerate for several days. Cut evenly into small squares to serve, or place in a storage container. The pemmican can be kept in a large block and pieces broken off as needed. This is a high-density food, and a small amount will be adequate. Although the ingredients in pemmican can be stored safely at room temperature, it is best to keep this in the refrigerator until ready to use.

Frozen Desserts

Frozen desserts with *Aronia* are a perfect way to have a healthy snack/dessert. Since the berry is not exposed to high heat, light, or an alkaline environment the healthy attributes are protected.

Ice cream/yogurt makers come in a variety of choices, from the original hand crank models that need ice to the electric-driven paddle types with gel-contained bowls. Regardless of the method used to freeze these treats, successful freezing will occur if the mixture is placed in a container in the freezer for about 30 minutes before pouring it into the ice cream/yogurt maker.

Frozen *Aronia* Yogurt—Makes 1 quart
2 cups vanilla low-fat yogurt
2 containers (5.3 ounce each) Greek-style vanilla yogurt
½ cup castor sugar
3 tablespoons honey or agave nectar
1 cup *Aronia* berries, fresh or frozen chopped coarsely
2 teaspoons lemon rind, grated

Combine all ingredients and mix well until blended. Pour into an ice cream maker and freeze according to directions. Serve after processing or place in a covered container in the freezer to create a firmer frozen yogurt. Chocolate sauce makes a wonderful topping for frozen *Aronia* yogurt.

Chocolate Sauce—Makes 1 serving
2 tablespoons chocolate syrup or hot fudge sauce
1 tablespoon *Aronia* juice
¼ teaspoon cinnamon

If using the hot fudge sauce, melt it in the microwave for about 30 seconds to soften. Add the juice and cinnamon to the sauce or syrup. Stir to combine and pour over the frozen dessert or sliced pears or strawberries.

<u>Granita—Serves 5 or 6</u>

A granita is a very delicate ice which helps to cleanse the palate. It could be served prior to the entrée or for a light dessert. A novel way to serve this frozen treat is to halve an orange, remove the filling, and use the shell as a bowl for the granita. You may need to slice off a small piece at the bottom of the outside to help the orange sit flat on a plate. Top with a sprig of refreshing mint.

2 (14-ounce) cans whole berry cranberry sauce
½ cup *Aronia* berries, fresh or frozen
2½ cups water
½ cup sugar or sugar substitute equivalent
3 teaspoons *Aronia* bitters or vodka (recipe in Beverages chapter)

Place the cranberry sauce and *Aronia* berries in a blender and process until the berries are chopped coarsely. Pour the berry mixture into an 8-quart saucepan and add the water and sugar. Heat the mixture on medium-low heat and stir until the sugar has dissolved. Remove the pan from the heat and allow to cool before adding the bitters or vodka. The granita mixture can be processed in an ice cream/ yogurt /sorbet maker or in a freezer-proof pan. If using the pan method, allow the mixture to begin to freeze. Remove the pan from the freezer and stir/scrape the mixture with a fork. Repeat every hour until coarse crystals have formed. When the process is finished, put it in an airtight freezer container and seal.

<u>*Aronia* Sorbet—Serves 5 or 6</u>
2 cups apple juice, unsweetened
1 cup sugar
1 cup *Aronia* berries, fresh or frozen, chopped coarsely
2 cups raspberries, fresh or frozen
1 cup orange juice (without pulp)

Combine the apple juice and sugar in a saucepan. Heat over medium-high heat for 3–5 minutes while stirring to dissolve the sugar and make a syrup. Remove from the heat and allow to cool for 5-10 minutes. Pour the cooled syrup and remaining ingredients into a food processor. If the berries are frozen, allow them to defrost to room temperature first. Process all ingredients on high until the mixture is smooth. Strain this mixture through a fine sieve to remove the seeds from the mixture. Refrigerate the mixture until chilled and then freeze in an ice cream/sorbet maker according to directions.

Berry Ice—Serves 5 or 6
1½ cups strawberries, fresh or frozen/partially thawed
½ cup *Aronia* berries, fresh or frozen/partially thawed
½ cup honey
2 tablespoons lemon juice

Place partially thawed berries and remaining ingredients in a blender. Blend on high speed for a minute or until the mixture is smooth. The mixture can be placed in an ice cream maker to freeze or in an 8x8-inch loaf pan. If using the pan method, allow the mixture to begin to freeze. Remove the pan from the freezer and stir/scrape the mixture with a fork every 15–20 minutes. Keep covered with foil.

Aronia Sherbet—Serves 5 or 6
2 cups *Aronia* berries
2 cups castor sugar
1 cup cream
2 cups milk, 1 percent or 2 percent
3 tablespoons lemon juice, freshly squeezed
1 tablespoon crystallized ginger, finely chopped

Combine the sugar, cream, and milk in a saucepan. Heat on medium-low stirring frequently until the sugar dissolves. Remove from the heat and allow the mixture to cool. Pour the cooled mixture into a blender. Add the *Aronia* berries and process on high until the berries are finely chopped. Add the lemon juice and crystallized ginger and pulse on low to blend all ingredients. Process according to the directions in an ice cream maker.

⌘ ⌘ ⌘

Aronia—On the Outside from Head to Toe

There are no known studies on the use of *Aronia* as a skin product. But…why not? Consumers pay dearly for skin products with high antioxidant qualities to protect and heal the skin. *Aronia* is a perfect product for such use, and it can be grown right in your backyard.

The products in this skin care section use readily available ingredients and may or may not have the addition of essential oils for fragrance. Many have an acidulant as a major ingredient, which also assists in preservation of the product and the berry's beneficial qualities. Added coloring is not necessary since the *Aronia* imparts a gentle purplish hue.

Hair Rinse

Beer has long been used as a hair rinse. It is actually nourishing to the hair and gives it body and sheen. The acidic qualities of the *Aronia* juice help to keep the pH of the scalp and hair in balance.

Combine 1 cup of flat beer with 1 cup of *Aronia* juice. Berry beers have an especially nice scent. In the winter 1 teaspoon of olive oil can be added as a moisturizer. Store the mixture in a plastic bottle. To use, mix 1 tablespoon of the beer/*Aronia* mixture with 2 cups water. Pour the mixture evenly through the hair. Use the rinse as a final rinse without rinsing out.

Fun Hair Streaks

Why not? No more synthetic dye for Halloween. Use a cotton swab or paint brush to color streaks on the hair with *Aronia* juice. It gives the hair an iridescent purple glow while conditioning. The color rinses out without leaving a trace.

Facial Mask

¼ cup oatmeal, quick cooking or regular
¼ cup yogurt, plain
1 tablespoon *Aronia* bits, dehydrated, or dehydrated *Aronia* pomace

Combine all ingredients in a food processor and blend until a smooth paste is created. A small amount of honey can be added to the mixture and blended to create a lighter facial mask. Apply the mask in a thin coat on the face and neck while avoiding the area around the eyes. Leave the mask on for 10 to 15 minutes, then rinse with slightly warm water. Blot your face with a clean cloth. Keep the mask refrigerated in a small, covered container. **Warning—do not answer the door while undergoing this treatment.**

<u>Lip Gloss</u>
　　1 tablespoon petroleum jelly
　　½ teaspoon *Aronia* juice

Simply blend the two ingredients. Use a cotton-tipped swab to put on your lips. Store in a small plastic pot. This gives quite a bit of color but is a nice treatment for the lips.

<u>Bath Fizzies, Lotions, Scrubs, Lip Balms</u>

There are several wonderful recipes for these items online. Making your own allows you to control the ingredient quality and quantity. Personal preferences for scents or unscented can be your choice. If you want to incorporate *Aronia*, it is important to look for recipes that have either oil or water as an ingredient. *Aronia* juice can easily be substituted for the water. The oil can be an infusion with *Aronia*. To make the infusion, choose a cosmetic-quality oil such as sweet almond or grapeseed. Heat 16 ounces of oil with 1 cup of chopped *Aronia* berries. The microwave can be used for this step with the power level on 50 percent. Stir every 2 minutes and remove after it becomes warm. The length of time will vary with the starting temperature of the oil. Pour the berry/oil mixture into a blender and pulse until the berries are completely blended with the oil. There will be some remaining pieces, so it is important to strain the oil through a fine mesh sieve. Pour the strained oil back into the original container until ready to use.

The ingredients will affect the final color of the product. Most fizzies maintain the berry color but some scrubs become more bluish as a result of the pH change.

Aronia *Fabric Dye*

Plants have been used as a natural dye for thousands of years. Leaves, bark, flowers, roots, and berries all have entered the dye pot in most cultures. *Aronia* berries impart a spectacular purplish hue that makes them especially desirable for a fabric dye. Successful fabric dyeing with *Aronia* requires a natural fabric, a pretreatment mordant (a substance used to set dyes), and proper dye techniques. Either the complete yardage can be dyed or the dye can be used for tie-dye. Natural dyes are more fragile with laundering procedures. Plus, *Aronia* does not respond well to contact with any metals or alkaline products, such as soap. The most beautiful purple fabric will become grey if it has contact with either. As a result, the most suitable uses would be fabric for bags, pillows, scarves, hats, vests, or other items that do not receive washings. If cleaning is necessary, dry cleaning is best so the color does not change.

The fabric: Natural fabrics (muslin, cotton, silks, and wool) in white or off-white colors are the best choices for dyeing. Some fabric stores have bolts of ready-to-dye cotton available. All 100 percent cotton fabrics will have some shrinkage. It is important to calculate for shrinkage when determining the amount of fabric to dye for your project. And if you are using wool, be mindful that it will shrink during the boiling stage and your fabric piece will be about 50 percent of the original size. But, you will have a beautiful piece of *Aronia*-colored boiled wool. It is best to prepare the dye solution before proceeding with the actual dye process. The dye solution can be stored in a jar at room temperature, but it needs to be used within several hours or it will begin to darken.

Testing the fabric: If you are not certain of the fiber content of your fabric, it is important to test the fabric, since a synthetic fabric does not dye well with natural dye. Synthetic fabrics are made with a solution where the dye is incorporated into the liquid before being pressed through a spinneret. To test the fabric, cut a small square. Holding the piece of fabric with metal tongs, let the fabric make contact with the flame of a candle. (It's advisable to have a piece of foil under the candle and all flammable items away from the flame.) Protein fibers such as wool, alpaca, angora, silk, and cotton will burn with a gray smoke and smell like burning hair. Synthetic fibers will usually have a black smoke and smell "chemical." The synthetic fabric sometimes leaves a hard residue, too.

Preparing the fabric to receive the dye: Most manufactured fabrics have a finish added at the end of the weaving or knitting stage to add luster, brightness, texture, or other desirable characteristics. These finishes coat the fabric fibers and do not allow complete absorption of the dye. To remove all finishes, the fabric must be pretreated with a mordant. Even fabrics labeled ready-to-dye should be pretreated to ensure even dyeing. The treatment can be made with a soda ash (soda carbonate) solution or salt solution. Usually the salt solution is recommended for berry dyes. Both solutions should use only purified water. Minerals present in water can affect the color of the dye.

A test was conducted to determine the effect of mordant and additive (lemon juice and alum) combinations with the *Aronia* dye. Samples of cotton, silk, and wool were used in six tests. The following chart describes the treatment for each sample:

A1 Salt fixative—berry dye	B1 Soda ash fixative—berry dye
A2 Salt fixative—berry dye plus alum	B2 Soda ash fixative—berry dye plus alum
A3 Salt fixative—berry dye plus lemon juice	B3 Soda ash fixative—berry dye plus lemon juice

The photo located in this book's center demonstrates the variance in colors obtained with the six different treatments. Alum (aluminum sulfate) and lemon juice are both acidic and will lower the pH of the dye solution. However, the color varies with both additives and mordants. The fabrics treated with the soda ash mordant have a slightly more reddish quality. The alum addition created a purplish dye in both mordants. The less appealing color was the salt fixative and lemon juice combination. This fabric has a yellow-green tinge. The silk is the most receptive to the dye, and the natural sheen enhances the color.

Making the mordant: The salt mordant can be made by combining 8 cups of purified water with ½ cup noniodized table salt. The solution should be brought to a boil. Add the fabric and simmer for 60 minutes. Let the fabric cool down in the pot, then remove the piece from the solution and rinse with cool water until the water is clear. This amount is enough for 1 yard of cotton or silk, but more will be needed for wool.

Soda ash for this method can be found in art/craft stores and even some box stores in the art/craft section. Soda ash changes the pH of the fibers and will work with plant fibers as well as silk. It is not recommended for wool, however. To use, make a solution with 1 cup of soda ash to 1 gallon of warm water. Soak your fabric in this solution for 1 hour. Remove the fabric from the solution and wring the fabric to remove excess water. Do not rinse. *Please*: complete this process wearing latex or nitrile gloves. If the solution contacts your skin, rinse with water as soon as possible!

Dye Bath: The amount of dye needed is dependent on the yardage and fabric thickness. Before beginning the process, it is best to wet the fabric and place it in the pan you intend to use. Mark the height of the fabric in the pan, remove the fabric, and fill the pan with water to calculate the necessary amount of dye.

Choose berries which are ripe and juicy to make the dye. Chop the berries and add to a nonreactive pan (an old enamel pot is ideal) with twice the amount of purified water, a 1:2 ratio. Bring the mixture to a boil and simmer for an hour with the lid on. Strain the dye to remove the berry solids by pouring first through a mesh strainer and then through a colander lined with three or four layers of cheesecloth. The mesh strainer will catch the large particles while the cheesecloth will collect the finer berry pieces. It is important to have solid matter removed from the juice for the dye since the berry pieces can cause spotting on the fabric. Pour the dye into a nonreactive pan (aluminum, copper, and iron pans will change the color, as will a metal spoon) and place the prepared fabric into the berry dye solution. Place the pan on the stove and heat over medium-low heat, stirring frequently. The fabric should remain immersed in the dye solution. Heat for about 20 minutes or until the desired color is reached. When the color has been obtained, remove the fabric from the solution and rinse in cool water until the water runs clear. Keep in mind that the fabric will dry to a lighter value. *Do not wring the fabric.* The fabric can be left in the container and allowed to sit in the dye overnight for a darker intensity of color. Allow the dyed fabric piece to air dry on a rack or bath towel bar. When dry the piece can be heat set with an iron on medium.

Aronia *for Our Four-Legged Friends*

Our four-legged friends will benefit from *Aronia* added to their meals or treats. Homemade treats allow you to control the ingredients and the size of the treat to control overfeeding. By making your own treats, you eliminate any food products that you know create a reaction for your pet. The addition of *Aronia* will provide your pet the same benefits that have been observed by humans who consume *Aronia*. Several research studies with rat and pig subjects have demonstrated lower toxicity levels in the liver and kidneys when being fed *Aronia*. Most domestic pets do not favor the whole raw berry but will consume the dehydrated form or pomace when mixed with their food or added to treats. It is always advised to consult with your veterinarian before making dietary changes for your pet. He or she can help you decide the amount to add to your pet's diet as well. Also, it is best to start the addition of *Aronia* slowly in small quantities as you would with any diet change for your pet. The recipes included in this section are a base for you to create additional foods for your pet.

Some foods should be avoided in domestic pet recipes at all times. Among these are:

- avocado
- chocolate
- coffee
- tea
- citrus oils
- grapes/raisins
- hops
- macadamia nuts
- mushrooms
- onions
- persimmons
- uncooked yeast dough
- xylitol

Dairy products may be a problem for some adult cats and dogs, so check with your vet before giving your pet these foods, too. Chocolate has an ingredient called theobromine, which is extremely toxic to pets. Symptoms include trembling, hyperactivity, and vomiting to mention a few. Macadamia nuts can create some of the same symptoms and even hyperthermia. Grapes and raisins are extremely toxic and may even lead to kidney damage or failure. And xylitol creates a fast release of insulin, which leads to hypoglycemia. Liver failure can be a result of xylitol ingestion, and even coma is a possibility. None of these ingredients should be added to pet food at any time, and our little friends need to be kept from accidental ingestion of these substances.

Biscuit Treats
1 egg
½ cup water
1 jar chicken and gravy baby food (2.5 ounces)
1 ¼ cups self-rising cornmeal mix
¼ cup dry milk
½ cup quick-cooking rolled oats
¼ cup wheat germ
¼ cup brewer's yeast
½ cup *Aronia* berries, dehydrated and coarsely chopped

Preheat the oven to 325°F. Prepare a cookie sheet with either parchment paper or a silicone mat, or grease lightly with shortening. In a small bowl, combine the egg, water, and baby food. Mix until well blended. In a large bowl, combine the remaining dry ingredients except the *Aronia* berries. Toss with a fork to mix all dry ingredients. Add the liquid ingredients to the dry ingredients and blend with a small hand mixer or wooden spoon. Add the *Aronia* bits and fold into the mixture.

The dough is very moist, but it can be patted on wax paper or parchment paper to ½-inch thickness or slightly less. Allow the dough to rest for 15–20 minutes. During the resting stage, the dry ingredients will absorb the moisture and the dough will be easier to cut. When the dough no longer has a shine, it can be shaped into treats. Use either a bone-shaped cookie cutter or other small cookie cutter, or cut by hand. Transfer the dough to a cutting board and use a pizza cutter or the flat end of a metal spatula to cut into dog-size bites. Place the cut treats onto the prepared cookie sheet and place in the center of the oven. Bake for 15 minutes, then turn off the heat (without opening the door) and let the biscuits remain in the oven for another 2½ hours. Since there are no preservatives in this recipe keep the biscuits stored in an airtight container in the refrigerator.

Frozen Treats for Man's Best Friend—Makes 12 to 14, 3ounce servings
1 quart vanilla low-fat yogurt
1 banana, mashed
3 tablespoons peanut butter, creamy and natural is best
2 tablespoons honey
¼ cup *Aronia* bits

Place all ingredients in a food processor and blend until the mixture is smooth. Pour the mixture into small paper cups, cover with foil or plastic wrap, and place in a level spot in the freezer. To serve, remove the paper cup from around the treat and place in the dog food dish. Use up to ½ cup of mixture for a very large dog and ¼ cup for a dog 25 pounds or less. If you want smaller treats, put the mixture into an ice cube tray and freeze. They can be popped out and kept stored in a freezer-proof container.

For the Birds…if you have made some oil infusions and don't want to throw away the strained berries, make a "cake" to put out for the birds in winter. Melt 1 cup crunchy peanut butter with ¾ cup of lard. To the melted mixture, add 2 cups quick-cooking oats, 2 cups cornmeal, 1 cup whole wheat flour, ⅓ cup sugar, and up to ½ cup of *Aronia* berries. Stir and pour into an 8x8-inch foil pan to freeze until ready to use. If the mixture is dry, add more melted lard, and add more flour if the mixture is too moist.

⌘ ⌘ ⌘

Glossary

Acidulants are substances that are acidic and have a low pH. Examples are acetic acid (vinegar), citric acid (juice from lemons and limes), malic acid (found naturally in apples, pears, tomatoes, bananas, and cherries), and tartaric acids (naturally produced in wine production).

Agave Nectar is from the agave plant, which is also the source for tequila. It is sweeter than sugar by 40 percent, so you can use less. Agave syrup also has a lower glycemic index than refined sugars, so it will not spike blood sugar levels like other sweeteners. Substitute ⅔ cup of agave syrup for every cup of sugar (white or brown). Reduce the liquids in the recipe by one fourth to one third. If using in baked goods, reduce the temperature by 25 degrees, but you may need to increase the baking time.

Anthocyanins are antioxidant flavonoids found in red/purplish fruits and vegetables. They have demonstrated abilities to act as a powerful antioxidant.

Antimutagenic is something that reduces or prevents mutations from occurring.

Antioxidants look for free radicals (ions, atoms and molecules in the body with unpaired ions thought by some to be responsible for certain diseases(and convert them to harmless substances in our body.

Antihyperglycemic is a substance which prevents elevated glucose levels.

Cardioprotective refers to heart protection.

Castor Sugar is a very fine granulated sugar. While it can be purchased in some stores under the description "superfine," it is simple to make by placing small quantities of regular granulated sugar in a food processor with the metal blade attachment and whirling until fine. Castor sugar is not the same as confectioner's sugar, which has added cornstarch.

Convection Baking is completed in a convection oven, which has a fan in the unit to move heat around the food while baking. Normally the temperature is reduced by 25 degrees from the conventional oven temperature.

Cultivar is a naming method for plants which have been cultivated specifically for specific characteristics.

Flavonoids are polyphenolic compounds created in some fruits, vegetables, legumes, and teas. They demonstrate promising results in reducing and preventing some diseases.

Free Radicals are unstable properties in our body which are created through various means. If they are excessive in the body, damage can occur to our cells.

Freezer-Proof containers provide a moisture and vapor barrier to food.

Hepatoprotective is an agent providing protection to the liver.

Low-fat is a food product which contains 3 grams or less of fat per serving.

Mordant is a substance used to help set dye in fabric. Berry dyes usually respond best to salt as a mordant. Other substances may affect the color outcome.

Nonreactive pans are those made from ceramic, glass, stainless steel, or Teflon-coated pans. Containers made from other materials may react with acidic foods.

Oxygen Radical Absorption Capacity (ORAC) is a method of measuring the ability of a substance to absorb free radicals. It was developed by the United States Department of Agriculture (USDA).

Pectin is a plant-based agent used to gel foods.

pH is a scale used to rate whether a substance is an acid or base. The range extends from 0 to 14 with 7 as neutral. The lower values are acidic and the higher values are alkaline.

Phytonutrient/Phytochemicals are used interchangeably and refer to compounds which may offer health protection.

Polyphenols act as antioxidants and may offer protection against some health conditions.

Pomace is the solid remains after pressing fruit. It has high nutritional value.

Tannin is a plant compound that is bitter and astringent in taste.

Xylitol is a sugar substitute extracted from plants.

⌘　⌘　⌘

Measure Equivalents

Cup	Fluid Ounces	Tablespoons	Teaspoons
1 c.	8 oz.	16 tbsp.	48 tsp.
¾ c.	6 oz.	12 tbsp.	36 tsp.
⅔ c.	5 oz.	11 tbsp.	33 tsp.
½ c.	4 oz.	8 tbsp.	24 tsp.
⅓ c.	3 oz.	5 tbsp.	15 tsp.
¼ c.	2 oz.	4 tbsp.	12 tsp.
⅛ c.	1 oz.	2 tbsp.	6 tsp.
¹⁄₁₆ c.	.5 oz.	1 tbsp.	3 tsp.

⌘　⌘　⌘

Recipe Index

Pet Treats

⌘ ⌘ ⌘

Note Page

Note Page

About the Author

Cheryl Saker has had an extensive career in education, teaching classes in the family and consumer science area. Health, foods/nutrition, international foods, adult education cooking classes are among the content areas in which she has expertise. She has developed curriculum using recipe development and nutritional analysis methodologies. After making a choice to stay home with young sons, she started a catering service. Upon returning to the classroom, she continued to coordinate catering projects for events, hosting up to a thousand people.

She received an undergraduate degree in family and consumer science from Bowling Green State University, Ohio, and a master's in career and technical education from the University of Nebraska. A lifelong learner, she continued to raise the bar for professional improvement and earned the National Board for Professional Teaching Standards Certification in career and technical education.

Following retirement from teaching, the author pursued her interest in horticulture by taking classes and entering the Master Gardener training program with the University of Nebraska Cooperative Extension. During this period she began research on the *Aronia melanocarpa* Michx. berry and realized the dynamic health qualities of this berry. As a result, the crop has become a family endeavor with over two thousand shrubs planted in southwest Iowa.

Made in the USA
Charleston, SC
17 August 2011